FIRST TO A MILLION

First to a Million: A Teenager's Guide to Achieving Early Financial Freedom

Dan Sheeks

Published by BiggerPockets Publishing LLC, Denver, CO

Copyright © 2021 by Dan Sheeks

All Rights Reserved.

Publisher's Cataloging-in-Publication Data

Names: Sheeks, Daniel Brian, 1974-, author.

Title: First to a million : a teenager's guide to achieving early financial freedom / by Dan Sheeks.

Description: Includes bibliographical references. | Denver, CO: BiggerPockets Publishing, 2021.

Identifiers: LCCN: 2021935113 | ISBN: 9781947200463 (paperback) | 9781947200470 (ebook)

Subjects: LCSH Teenagers--Finance, Personal. | Investments. | Finance, Personal. | BISAC YOUNG ADULT NONFICTION / Business & Economics | YOUNG ADULT NONFICTION / Inspirational & Personal Growth | YOUNG ADULT NONFICTION / Personal Finance

Classification: LCC HG4527 .S54 2021| DDC 332.63/22/0835--dc23

Published in the United States of America

10 9 8 7 6 5 4 3 2 1

FIRST TO A MILLION

A TEENAGER'S GUIDE to Achieving Early Financial Freedom

BY DAN SHEEKS

BiggerPockets® PUBLISHING
Denver, Colorado

DEDICATION:

To my son, Callum, and all the other young people who may someday read this book. I sincerely hope you find it helpful in the pursuit of your best life.

and to the ORIGINAL FI FREAKS:

Jabbar Adesada
Kaitlin Becker
Kade Brunson
Aden Brust
Damon Cameron Jr
Sannibel Carter
Benjamin Carver
Ali Chauhan
Leo Chun
Luke Engelby
Ben Firstenberg
Bryant Francom
Jacob Frenzen
Ethan Gregerson
Alexandra Gruitch
Chase Guelette

Joseph Hartley
Aiden Hatchett
Henry Huang
Tamirah Jackson
Dani Kaur
Abby Link
Joe Mannino
Thomas Martinez
JT Marting
Caden McBride
Katalina Mendoza
Elizaveta Nagornaia
Greg Oliver III
Saketh Pabolu
Jacob Pieczynski
Alex Pierce

Nick Pierce
Caxie Primacio
Izayah Pulido
JD Randall
Carson Smith
William Spence
Marcel Sunday
Logan Taylor
Sam Tecun
Taylor Thompson
Terry Turner
Sarah Zdanowski
Josiah Zebarth
Ben Zelenka

TABLE OF CONTENTS

PART 1
THE STANDARD PATH AND A DIFFERENT OPTION

PART 2
THE FI FOUNDATION

PART 3
THE KEYS TO FI

FOREWORD

The journey to achieving financial independence is different for everyone.

Back when I was in high school, I had never heard of financial independence. There were no influencers or content creators talking about it. (The term "influencer" hadn't even been coined yet!) Social media platforms like Facebook and YouTube were just getting started—Instagram and TikTok probably weren't even a thought yet. It's not surprising, then, that I had never heard of the concept until around 2013 when I was working as a substitute teacher.

Now, I'll admit that I was not a very good substitute teacher. My version of teaching was taking roll, turning on a video for the class, and sitting back to read a book. One week, someone recommended I read a book called *Rich Dad Poor Dad* by Robert Kiyosaki. I picked it up with no knowledge and minimal expectations; little did I know that reading that book would drastically change how I viewed money and freedom. For the first time in my life, I was aware of financial independence—and I wanted to figure out how to get there!

Fast forward to 2021.
In just eight years, my life has changed dramatically. I've built multiple companies that have made me millions of dollars. I've purchased hundreds of homes and established a diversity of passive income streams. There are a lot of ways people succeed in this world. But I can say with certainty that the only reason I was able to accomplish those things is that I was willing to seek out the right information.

With the help of fantastic resources like BiggerPockets, I closed on my first real estate deal. I networked and found mentors who guided me as my business grew. I sought out brilliant business partners who filled in the gaps where I lacked. But most importantly, I found people who inspired me to think bigger and achieve more. Thanks to social media, I never met many of these inspiring people face-to-face; I've been able to watch and learn from them through their online platforms.

It was social media that introduced me to Dan (and led to me writing this foreword). Initially, Dan reached out to me about getting on a Zoom call with his group of teenage entrepreneurs. I didn't know what to expect on the call, and I was shocked to see how far they were in their journey!

These young people were doing things that I hadn't learned until my 20s—and even my 30s! Many of them were already making thousands of dollars through side hustles. I couldn't believe it when I found out that one of those side hustles was something called "couch flipping"—a project I was very familiar with, since I had popularized it on my YouTube channel and the *BiggerPockets Real Estate Podcast!* Seeing first-hand in Dan's students how financial education pays off—literally—was a tremendous experience. It was so cool that these teenagers were already so far ahead of where I was at their age.

Now, you may not yet be a part of this elite group of teenagers, but everything you need to succeed is right here in this book. It took me years to learn the lessons that Dan shares so well.

(That's probably why he's a real teacher, and I was just a substitute.)
One of my favorite aspects is the Four Mechanisms of Early FI.

1. Earn more.

2. Spend less.

3. Save the difference.

4. Invest your savings wisely.

Earning more money is the hard part for most people. The path to that financial destination looks different for different people. For some, it may be something drastic, like changing careers. Others may find success in one of the many side hustles that Dan suggests throughout this book. But no matter what, your journey starts with finding a way to earn more income.

Next, you have to be disciplined enough to spend less than you currently do—even though you're making more money! It sounds crazy, because the typical reason we want to make more money is to have a better lifestyle. A bigger house, a nicer car, better clothes—we've been taught our whole lives to aspire to this lifestyle and everything that comes with it. But those who are dedicated to achieving early financial independence are willing to wait for these things. There's nothing wrong with having nice stuff (and your definition of "nice stuff" may vary), but true discipline is knowing how to avoid lifestyle inflation. A FI Freak knows that the most important lifestyle to aspire to is *freedom*—and the happiness that comes with it.

After learning discipline and spending less, you now need to save that money. Building up a reserve account will help you in your time of need and give you the peace of mind that comes with knowing you've got a safety net. I'm much more focused, happy, and productive when I have that margin in my life. You will be too!

The last step is to invest those savings wisely. There are so many investment opportunities in today's world. With social media, it seems like all of them can make you rich quickly. But the reality is most investments take time to produce. This is where that discipline you learned comes back into play. You'll need to find your investing niche and go all-in on understanding it. I've made my wealth by investing in real estate and my businesses. I'm not a very good stock trader or crypto trader, and that's okay. Being great at one thing can make you a lot of money—being mediocre at many things . . . not so much!

These four steps sound simple in theory, but the truth is if you neglect just one of them, it screws up the whole plan. But there is hope.

The fact that you are reading this right now shows that you are far ahead of your peers. I want to encourage you to use this to your advantage. Take the things you learn in this book and apply them immediately. Many people fall into the trap of waiting for the perfect time before they take action. Here's the truth . . .

There is no perfect time. The time is now!

Just like *Rich Dad Poor Dad* changed my mentality, *First to a Million* will change how you think about money, your values, and what freedom is.

I'll let Dan take it from here.

Best,
Ryan Pineda

Pronounced "fye," like FI-re.

FINANCIAL INDEPENDENCE, OR FI:
The point at which someone no longer needs to work for money, also referred to as financial freedom.

FREAK:
1. A person who has withdrawn from normal behavior and activities to pursue one interest or obsession.

2. One who is markedly exceptional or extraordinary.

If you are a young person obsessed with making intelligent financial decisions, allowing yourself to reach early financial independence and live your best life, then you are different.
YOU ARE EXCEPTIONAL.
YOU ARE UNIQUE.
YOU ARE A FI FREAK!

Take a selfie with the cover of this book and post it all over your social media accounts with **#TEENAGEFIFREAK** and **#FREAKDAY1.**

By notifying others that you are starting your journey to early financial independence, you will be held more accountable to your goals.

Make sure to tag **@BIGGERPOCKETS** and **@SHEEKSFREAKS!**

INTRODUCTION

Make no mistake about it: This book is *not* about money.

It is about freedom, choices, opportunities, and—most of all—happiness.

The title of this book, *First to a Million*, will mean different things to different readers. "A million" could refer to a million dollars of income or a million-dollar net worth. Some of you might be thinking of number of followers, likes, subscribers, comments, or retweets. It could also refer to connections or accomplishments. But for *everyone* who reads this book, "a million" signifies a different kind of mindset when it comes to achieving and succeeding. If you're taking the time to read this book, you are intensely interested in reaching goals most would never even consider—like early financial independence, or FI.

Achieving FI early in life is not normal. It's exceptional. As a matter of fact, it's *Freakish*. To achieve this sort of freedom, you must be willing to do things most people your age would never consider. Therefore, you will need to get comfortable with being different. As you read this book and adopt its ideas and strategies, you will ultimately transform into a FI Freak. Let me be the first to welcome you to our community. Life is good here!

You may be reading this book because a trusted adult in your life gave it to you. If so, I recommend reading the entire book as a token of your appreciation for this adult and the fact that they have your best interest in mind.

You may have found this book on your own. If so, that is impressive!

Knowing this book will cover topics like money, personal finance, investing, and retirement, you have voluntarily agreed to give it a shot. That is *not* normal for someone your age. See, you are already Freakish—and that's a good thing!

Whether you bought this book for yourself or got it from someone else, commit to reading it with an open mind. When you're done, ask yourself these questions:

- Is this something that can help me?
- Is this something I want to pursue?
- Is this something I'm willing to work hard for?

This book's purpose is to provide you with more options for your future, but which option you choose will ultimately be *your* decision. If you do decide to pursue early FI, your journey will present opportunities and choices you can't even dream of today. However, it's up to you to make the most of your future—nobody else can do the work for you.

The first step is to read this book. Then, if early FI becomes a goal for you, use the step-by-step guide called the FI Freak Checklist located in Appendix A. Learn as much as you can. Ask questions. Achieve your goals. Give back. And always preserve the unique attitude that allows you to thrive and achieve.

Why It's Good to Be a FI Freak

Freaks are the much-needed escape from the humdrum. They are poetry.

—ATTRIBUTED TO ALBERT PERRY

1. A person who has withdrawn from normal behavior and activities to pursue one interest or obsession.

2. One who is markedly exceptional or extraordinary.

 1. A young person obsessed with making intelligent money decisions to allow themselves to reach early financial independence and live their best life.

Very few young people choose to think about their financial future, so being a FI Freak is not typical. If you are one of the few who fall into this category, you *are* Freakish. You are extraordinary and different. Accept it, appreciate it, and capitalize on it.

A FI Freak is also someone who doesn't subscribe to these commonly accepted life rules:

- You must work for forty-plus years.
- To be successful, you must go to college.
- You must own a beautiful luxury car and a big house.
- Personal finance is complicated.
- You must look wealthy to be wealthy.
- You should spend all the money you make.

If you decide to pursue early FI, you should know that others probably won't understand the decisions you'll be making. They will notice some of the extraordinary things you're doing and wonder why you're doing them. Some will ask you about it. Others will tease you about it. And others may even criticize you. Please take this advice from my good friend Craig Curelop:

> As you embark on your journey toward financial independence, realize that you are signing up for a life that is against societal norms. The first few years will feel like a sacrifice, but know that the remaining years will be well worth it … My advice would be to confidently embrace it. People are going to question and joke around with you about your [Freakishness]. Be confident and know that your strategy will work and that these same people who were questioning you will one day be envying you.

The Purpose of *First to a Million*

The FI strategy gives you power. It gives you the ability to take control of your life.

—BRAD BARRETT ON THE CHOOSEFI PODCAST, EPISODE 072R
@CHOOSEFIRADIO ▶ CHOOSEFI

My primary purpose in writing this book is to provide teens with options for how to live their lives—numerous and abundant options, which most Americans do *not* have because they must work to earn that next paycheck to pay their bills. This book is designed to explain specific methods of earning extra income, saving money, and investing that will put you on track to reach early FI. *First to a Million* will explore the fundamentals and most important topics you'll need for your journey. Then you can follow the steps in the FI Freak Checklist.

We will cover subjects most teenagers don't want to think, learn, talk, or read about. Subjects like personal finance, investing, saving, long-term goals, and retirement couldn't be more off-putting to a typical teen. The average teen, if given this book, would never even open it.

Since you *are* reading this, you have opened the door to changing your life for the better. You now have the option to save yourself from having to work a job until your hair is gray. Instead, you can get to a point in life where you get up each day and say, "What is it I truly want to do today that will make me happy and help others?" without worrying about having the time or money to do so.

The Origins of *First to a Million*

In 2016, my fiancée (now wife) and I really started to get interested in real estate investing and early FI. We both had owned a rental property or two before meeting each other and were diligent about properly managing our finances. When we combined forces, our common interest multiplied. It was like one plus one equaled five. (Although I must give credit where credit is due—my wonderful wife was the driving force in the beginning and brought more to the table than I did.)

I've always been interested in personal finance and entrepreneurship. (That's probably why I became a high school business teacher.) When I met my wife, she was already following BiggerPockets, an online community for any and all people interested in real estate investing, building wealth, and achieving early FI. I was instantly hooked and quickly learned as much as I could about money and real estate investing.

Because the BiggerPockets headquarters is in Denver, Colorado, near where we live, we had the opportunity to go to a meetup there. We registered online and were excited to mingle with members of the BiggerPockets community at the event: 100–200 people who were *all* interested in early FI and real estate investing. We had finally found our squad.

As the event was winding down and my wife and I were deciding whether we should head home, a young man introduced himself and we started chatting. He had on a BiggerPockets T-shirt, so I asked him if he worked there. Lo and behold, he had just moved from California because he had been offered a finance job at BiggerPockets.

His name was Craig Curelop, a 25-year-old who I later discovered was absolutely crushing it. He had just bought his first property, a duplex in Denver, using a strategy called "house hacking." If done well, this strategy (which we'll talk about later) pays for the property's expenses— meaning the owner gets to live in the property for *free*.

Craig rented out one side of the duplex and lived in the other, but because Craig is a bona fide FI Freak, he didn't stop there! The half he lived in was a one-bedroom unit, and he decided to make even more money by renting out his bedroom to guests through Airbnb. When he had guests, which was almost every night, he would sleep on a futon in the living room. Between the rent from the second-unit tenants and the money from Airbnb rentals of his own bedroom, Craig was bringing in much more money than the total expenses of the property. He was getting *paid* to live there.

Beyond his creative living situation, Craig was also crushing it by earning extra income with side hustles (e.g., he was an Uber driver for a while), using various frugal tactics (he would ride his bike everywhere possible rather than drive his car), and saving a boatload of money in the process. This allowed him to buy another rental property just a year later.

Knowing all this about Craig, I later asked him to speak to one of my high school business classes about his side hustles, frugality, and real estate experiences. I knew my students would relate to Craig since, at age 25, he was just a few years older than them. Needless to say, his visit to the class went extremely well. The students were in awe of his Freakish money decisions.

That summer, I asked Craig if he would be willing to speak to my students regularly over the next school year. He agreed, and we made an initial plan for him to come in about once a month. He also mentioned that his boss, Scott Trench, might be interested in coming to some of the classes too.

Scott, who was 28 at the time, had joined the BiggerPockets start-up early in 2014 and was actually the company's third employee. (These days, he's the president and CEO of BiggerPockets, managing more than forty employees.) Like Craig, he was also house hacking a property he had bought in Denver. One day that summer, the three of us met for beers and laid out a plan for them to talk to my senior business class about all the strategies they were using to achieve early FI.

Throughout that school year, Craig and Scott regularly came into my classroom. The students loved their visits and became super curious about early FI, frugality, and investing. During a visit in the fall of 2018, Craig and Scott were winding down the conversation with the students as the bell was about to ring. Scott asked *them* a question that changed everything for me: "When Craig and I come back, what do you want us to talk about?"

One of my students responded, "I get all of this. It makes sense to me, and it sounds like a good idea. But I just want someone to tell me what to do and keep it simple. What *exactly* should I do over the next couple of years, and when should I do it?"

That question resonated with me.

It also generated the idea of a checklist that would make it easy for my students to work toward early FI. (The result is—you guessed it—the FI Freak Checklist located in Appendix A.) I also realized that if I wanted other teens, beyond my students, to succeed in using this tool, I needed a book to explain the basic financial planning principles behind it.

The goal of writing *First to a Million* was born.

How to Use This Book

First to a Million introduces topics and strategies that are essential for your journey to early FI. Reading this book is the first step you need to take to get started, as it explains basic concepts for a successful path to early FI.

Throughout the book, you will see definitions labeled "Freak Speak." These are terms and strategies that are important to understand on your FI Freak journey. As the book introduces new topics and ideas, make sure to seek additional information if those topics or ideas aren't clear to you. If needed, Google the topic or search for it on YouTube to seek out other viewpoints.

The book also includes case studies of Featured Freaks. These will highlight real people who have either completed their journey to FI or are well on their way. And they *all* did it when they were young. They are proof that the concepts and strategies in this book work—if you are totally ready to commit.

In addition to this book, you can use the FI Freak Checklist in Appendix A. Once you finish reading this book, use this checklist to guide you through the actions you should be taking over the next few years. The checklist is all you'll need to move forward.

As we wrap up the introduction of this book, take a selfie with the cover of this book and post it all over your social media accounts with the hashtags #teenagefifreak and #freakday1, which will help keep you accountable to the people you know. And don't forget to tag @biggerpockets and @sheeksfreaks so these communities can cheer you on!

This is Day 1 of your FI Freak journey. You will *never* have another opportunity to take a selfie on Day 1. Someday you will look back at your Day 1 selfie and say to yourself, "That was the most important day of my life."

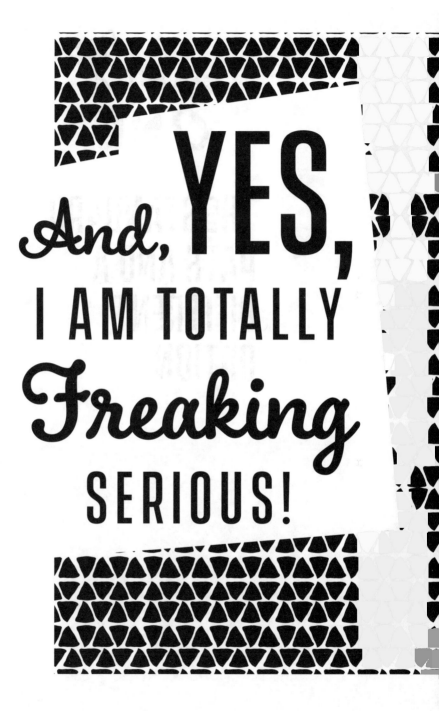

And, **YES,**
I AM TOTALLY
Freaking
SERIOUS!

PART ONE

THE STANDARD PATH AND A DIFFERENT OPTION

Don't think of what's possible with what you have today. Think of what's possible. Period. Then figure out what you need to get there.

—BRANDON TURNER ON THE BIGGERPOCKETS PODCAST, EPISODE 400
@BEARDYBRANDON @BEARDYBRANDON

Part One is all about learning the basics. What *is* financial independence, and why should you care?

In Chapter One, we will begin your journey by examining the fundamental benefits of early FI and why you might want to achieve it. We will then dive into the FIRE (Financial Independence, Retire Early) movement, tackling the idea of "retirement" and what it really means.

In Chapter Two, we will examine the typical American Dream path. We will explore what parts of it do and don't work in today's world and why it's likely not the best plan for you. We will also look at what having a job really entails and why so many Americans get trapped in theirs.

Finally, in Chapter Three, I will define FI, present the FI Equation, and introduce the Four Mechanisms of Early FI, which are the key to your financial freedom.

Let's get started!

CHAPTER 1:
AN INTRODUCTION TO FINANCIAL INDEPENDENCE

A boss takes one of his top salespeople, Jimmy, out to the company parking lot.

The boss says, "Look at my gorgeous new Lamborghini! It has all the bells and whistles, and it's soooo fun to drive!"

Jimmy is blown away by the beauty of the car and is secretly jealous. He can't help but wonder how much a car like that must cost and if he would ever be able to afford one for himself.

The boss continues, "Jimmy, if you work really hard this year, if you do everything you're told to do, work lots of hours of overtime, and produce like an all-star for the company . . . I'm going to be able to buy myself another one next year too. So keep up the good work!"

We might smile at this anecdote, but there is nothing funny about it. If you take a minute to think about Jimmy's situation and who is benefiting from his hard work, it's actually pretty terrifying.

Jimmy is your average Joe. Fast-forward ten years, and you could be Jimmy. He's just living his life the way he's seen others living theirs. He's grinding down the pathway that many identify as the American Dream. But what nobody ever told Jimmy was that by following this path, he will work away the best years of his life to make someone *else* wealthy. He is not aware there are other options that can give him more freedom.

Now, you are free to go down Jimmy's route. In many ways, Jimmy's path works just fine. He's living a noble life. He's making good money working hard at a good job, and he'll do it until he's ready to retire at 65. There's nothing inherently wrong with that. Millions of people have used that same plan to live happy and fulfilling lives.

But you should know there are other options. Options that can involve earning more, spending less, investing intelligently, creating passive income, and being your own boss. Options that will allow you to save decades of your time. This book will explore those options. My challenge to you is to look at *all* the options, understand the pros and cons of each, and choose the path that best suits you and your future goals. That's the Freakish thing to do.

Why Pursue FI?

Those who attain financial freedom are beholden to no job, boss, or company. They are free to choose how they direct their day in its entirety, without the need to generate income. They are free to live life as it was meant to be lived.

—SCOTT TRENCH, SET FOR LIFE
@SCOTT_TRENCH

To understand why early FI is an idea worth exploring, you should know its most important benefit: You won't *have* to work anymore. Some will say this reason alone is enough, but there are many more reasons to pursue FI. We'll go over them in Chapter Six, when we take a look at the Why of FI.

For now, let's just focus on this fundamental benefit—not having to work. Obviously, when you do reach FI, you can choose to continue working, and many financially independent people do continue to work at a job they love. But the point is you have the *option* to work, or not.

Now, let's slow down just a minute and think about this. We are talking about being very young and having the option of whether or not to work. This is *huge*! It's a choice that very, very few people can even fathom, let alone achieve, until they are old and gray. It is downright Freakish. It's a big fat 10 on the FI Freak scale.

What is so surprising to most people is that achieving FI at a very early age *is* completely possible. Many have done it. Many others will do it. It takes work, but *you* can do it too.

To reach FI, however, you will need to have a job. That job will supply the money to fuel your journey until you reach FI.

Once you have reached FI, you will have these three options:

1. You can continue to work the job you have because: you love it, it's gratifying, you enjoy the people you work with, you want the extra cash to buy more investments, and/or some combination of these reasons.

2. You can quit your current job and get a different job that you might enjoy more. The new job could pay less than the old job—perhaps a lot less. But that's alright because you don't *need* the income from a job anymore. You are choosing to work because you want to.

3. You can elect not to have a job. When you choose this option, you will have a variety of satisfying alternatives to fill your time.

Controlling Your Time

The result [of achieving FI] is liberating your most precious resource—your time—to make room for more happiness, more freedom, and more meaning.

—VICKI ROBIN AND JOE DOMINGUEZ, *YOUR MONEY OR YOUR LIFE*
@VICKIROBIN

The most important benefit of not having to work is gaining control of how you spend your time.

When you have control over how you spend your time, a world of new possibilities opens up to you. Most people who have achieved FI at a young age start working on something else they are passionate about (like a better job, volunteering, starting a new business, or teaching others), which keeps them busy and fulfilled.

Do you know adults who lack the freedom of time? Are you afraid the need to work for money will control your life? We only have a finite amount of time, which is why it is our most precious resource. And as you advance in life, your remaining time becomes less and less, making it even more valuable. By reaching FI early in life, you have the ability to optimize your time, which allows you to live your best life.

Many people follow the typical American Dream path of getting a full-time job they may not even like and working until they are 65. They need to work that mediocre job because it pays the bills and gives them security. They spend all of their twenties working hard (sometimes more than sixty hours per week) to please the corporate boss so they may advance someday and earn a little more. But when their twenties are over, they look back and say, "Was that worth it? I just spent the best decade of my life working, working, and working some more. And now that my twenties are over, I must continue working for three or four more *decades*. Ouch!"

By reaching FI early, you will reclaim decades of your life. You will be rich with time. You will have countless options to fill your days since you will no longer *have* to work. Here are just a few possibilities:

- Continue working your job because you truly enjoy it
- Start a new business
- Spend more time with friends and family
- Volunteer
- Write
- Exercise more
- Explore a favorite hobby
- Start a family
- Learn something new
- Travel to amazing places
- Go on adventures

Of course, you could do one or two of these things even while working a full-time job, but imagine how many of them you could do if you freed up an extra forty to sixty hours per week!

When you are financially independent, the options are endless because you are rich with time. You can spend it however you want.

The FIRE Movement

Everybody uses the FIRE acronym because it is catchy, and "Early Retirement" sounds desirable. But for most people who get there, Financial Independence does not mean the end of your working career. Instead, it means, "Complete freedom to be the best, most powerful, energetic, happiest and most generous version of You that you can possibly be."

—MR. MONEY MUSTACHE, "WHAT EVERYBODY IS GETTING WRONG ABOUT FIRE," MR. MONEY MUSTACHE CLASSIC BLOG
@MRMONEYMUSTACHE ▶ MR. MONEY MUSTACHE

You may have heard of a personal finance movement called Financial Independence, Retire Early (or FIRE) that's been gaining attention lately. Just Google "FIRE movement" and you'll see numerous links to websites, podcasts, documentaries, magazine articles, books, and more. The movement has really picked up steam over the past five years, going from a few dozen followers to hundreds of thousands. And it's not finished growing—not even close.

The FIRE movement is all about making changes to how you live your life so you can achieve FI at a very early age. It is *not* a get-rich-quick scheme. It is *not* a multilevel marketing organization. It is *not* a too-good-to-be-true scam. And it is *certainly* not about cheating others to become wealthier.

The FIRE movement is about adopting proven methods to handle your finances so you can reach FI quicker than you would by following the typical American Dream path.

The FIRE community has grown so rapidly because many of its successful members have made their stories, advice, and strategies publicly available for free. Some FIRE members may charge $5 for an e-book or $15 for a hard-copy book, but they're not trying to scam anyone with those prices. (By the way, here's some crucial advice: If someone tries to sell you information, a course, a program, a seminar, or anything similar, and they're charging more than $50 for it, *run away as fast as you can!* There is no information they can give you that is not available online or somewhere else for free or a minimal price.)

Thousands of members of the FIRE community have proven that early FI is possible. Gone are the images of grandpa and grandma playing cards with friends and visiting the grandkids as the typical retirement profile. FIRE members as young as 25 are achieving FI, proving it can be done with determination and persistence. It does take hard work and sometimes sacrifice, but anyone willing to follow the path can achieve it.

Still, some people feel that the FIRE movement is unrealistic or a sham. Their articles and opinions are on the internet as well. I've found that those who speak out against the FIRE movement fall into one of three categories:

1. They tried the FIRE strategies but did not have the perseverance and commitment to follow through and reach FI. They just didn't have what it takes, so they choose to bad-mouth the whole movement.
2. They took it too far. In an effort to reach FI as quickly as they could, some individuals have gone to extremes, cutting out almost everything in life that costs money, including things they value. This makes it difficult to be happy. It was only a matter of time before they gave up.
3. They never gave the FI strategies a try. They fear going against the grain and making different choices. Denouncing the entire movement helps them justify their decision to do nothing.

What Is Retirement?

The word "retirement" brings a certain image to mind: A couple of grandparents sitting in their rocking chairs and enjoying the sunset from their front porch. Or maybe they're traveling, golfing, and fulfilling the dreams they put on hold until they retired. They are cheerful and relaxed since they don't ever have to report to work at 8 a.m. again. They seem well rested and content. Not a bad life they have—not bad at all.

Most of us think of "retired people" as those who have been around awhile. To put it bluntly, only *old* people get to retire.

I wanted to see if today's teens think of retirement this way. In 2019, I surveyed about a hundred of my high school juniors about work and retirement. Here are two of the questions I asked and the results:

What is the average age at which someone retires?

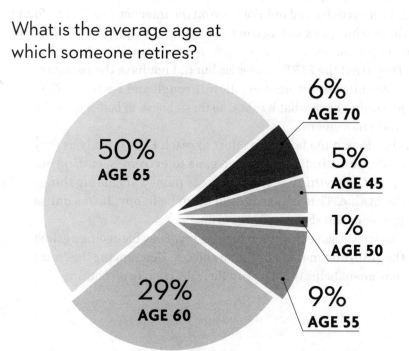

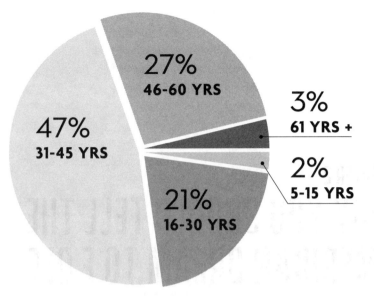

How many years does the average person spend working in their lifetime?

I asked these questions to see whether my students' ideas around work and retirement were the same as my generation's—and they were. Exactly half the juniors said the average retirement age was 65. And nearly half thought the average person spends thirty-one to forty-five years working. These results confirmed what I had suspected. Your generation believes what all previous generations have believed about work and retirement: You work until you're old, and only then can you retire.

Even though the word "retirement" appears in the FIRE acronym, please don't think that never working again is the path most choose to follow after achieving early FI.

Instead, most early FIers seek out other ways to contribute to society. Now, some of those ways could be considered "work." But when you do what you want, when you want, with whom you want, it doesn't feel like work—it is much more rewarding, fulfilling, and enjoyable. That is what you can look forward to if you proceed with your FI journey.

Those who are motivated enough to pursue the goal of early FI are generally not the type of people who will sit around relaxing all day and contribute nothing. They are FI Freaks, and they must keep *doing*.

CHAPTER 2:
WHY YOU SHOULD TELL THE AMERICAN DREAM TO F OFF

The problem with [the American Dream] is that the person following it will be forced to work… for the better part of his day, during the best part of his week, throughout the best years of his life. At best, he will retire with a modest amount of wealth, late in life, and be forced to hope it's enough to last.

—SCOTT TRENCH, *SET FOR LIFE*
@SCOTT_TRENCH

If you asked random people on the street to describe the typical American Dream pathway, the most common reply would sound something like this:

Go to high school, get a 3.7 GPA or better, go to college, get good grades, get a job, get married, get a dog, work for a good company, buy a beautiful luxury car, get a promotion, make a good salary, buy a lovely big house with a white picket fence, save a little money, have 2.3 kids, work long and hard hours, see your kids in the late evenings and on weekends, get another promotion, think about saving money to retire, get three weeks of vacation a year, take a trip to Disneyland with the family, work some more, send your kids to college, work till you're 65, retire, spend your seventies and eighties living the "good" life, play golf with your friends, visit your grandkids, travel to places you've always wanted to go, wonder how life went by so fast, die a peaceful death.

This exact plan has sufficed for millions. And, as I said before, there's nothing inherently wrong with it. It's a proven strategy—if you're okay with working into your sixties. But what nobody talks about are the *other* options.

Take this one, for instance:

Go to high school, graduate with a 1.5 GPA or better, start working and saving, find a side hustle to make even more money, live with your parents for a couple of years to save money, take the money you saved to buy a house when you're 20, house hack it (more on this later), save even more money, buy another property at age 21 and another at age 22, turn them into cash-flowing rental properties, invest some of the money generated from those properties in stock market index funds (more on this later too), invest the rest in more real estate, house hack another property at age 23 and again at 24, live a lifestyle that does not waste money, at a very young age realize that the passive income from your investments comes to more than your living expenses, recognize that this means you are financially independent, quit working for "the man," focus time on your investments and growing them, realize you are an entrepreneur and didn't even know it, keep growing your investments because you actually enjoy making money for yourself, get married, have 2.3 kids, buy a modest home and a dependable used car, take your family on vacations wherever and whenever you want, never miss one of your kids' recitals or games, spend your thirties and forties and fifties and sixties and seventies and eighties living the good life pursuing hobbies and interests that bring you joy, spend as much time as you can with your grandkids from the day they're born, die in a freak skydiving accident, leave your children a five-million-dollar real estate portfolio as an inheritance, drop the mic—peace out, world.

That's just *one* of the other options out there, but for some reason, it's not as well known as the typical American Dream pathway. Maybe because it's not the norm. Maybe because it's a little too Freakish.

This book's primary purpose is to examine *other* ways to live out the American Dream. If you choose the old-school version, that's okay. If you want to follow a path with a different version of happiness and fulfillment, that's okay too, and this book can be your guide. It's your choice, and there is no right or wrong answer.

The Truth About Jobs

What's so bad about having a job, anyway? Why would someone want to work hard at achieving FI just to avoid having to work? Let's dig into that a bit.

Imagine you just graduated from high school or college and landed your first real job. Since this is a long-term job for which you are highly qualified, you will be earning a yearly salary—let's say it's $50,000 a year. What does that really mean to you? To understand, you first need to think about how many hours are required to do this job.

If you think you'll work only forty hours per week, think again. A Gallup poll found that full-time salaried U.S. workers typically put in forty-nine hours per week. And that's the *average*. This includes many people who are in the latter half of their careers and have found ways to decrease that amount of time, sometimes out of necessity.

The truth is that most young workers find themselves working *more* than the average forty-nine hours per week. Companies often expect them to do this because young employees tend to be single with no kids and thus have fewer commitments. Also, new and young employees are more driven to make their boss or company happy since most are working their first job and want to succeed.

That same Gallup poll found that 25 percent of salaried workers put in more than *sixty hours* per week. I would guess most of those people were under 30 years of age.

Many companies entice fresh college grads with high salaries and then expect them to work *much* more than the typical forty hours a week. They won't say this outright, but they will tell you precisely what you must get done to be "good at your job," knowing that your workload will require more than those forty hours. If you are fortunate, your employer might pay overtime for those extra hours, but this usually applies just to hourly employees. (Also, overtime pay is only a good thing if you don't mind working the extra hours rather than doing something else with your valuable time.)

Let's suppose you took that job with a $50,000 yearly salary, you worked forty hours per week, and you received three weeks of vacation time per year. That would come out to $25.51 per hour [$50,000 ÷ {(52 weeks – 3 weeks) × 40 hours}]. That's pretty good compared to the average high school student's job that might pay between $12 and $15 an hour. However, if you end up needing to work sixty hours a week to be "good at your job," that comes out to earning $17.01 per hour. Eighty hours a week? That equals $12.76!

Is it worth being able to tell someone you make $50,000 a year when you have to work sixty hours a week—or more—just to do so? To work those long hours, what are you giving up that would make life more enjoyable? Most likely, you are sacrificing time with family and friends as well as your hobbies.

How high a salary would make giving up the things you enjoy worth it to you? The answer varies, but the sad part is that *nobody* gets asked that question. No employer says, "I will pay you $50,000 a year, but you'll have to work sixty hours a week, which means you will have less time to spend with your family and friends and on your hobbies. Do you want the job?"

People just find themselves in a job that requires a substantial time commitment, and then slowly, their happiness takes a back seat. This is the ugly downside of the typical American Dream pathway.

FI Freaks know they can use early FI to break out of this cycle.

But why should you, a teenager, worry about pursuing FI? You probably haven't finished high school yet, let alone started your first real job. It's difficult for you to visualize what it would be like to do the so-called "9-to-5 until you're 65" grind for forty-plus years.

The best way to gain some insight into that world might be to look at your parents. Do they work from Monday through Friday from nine to five (or until six or seven, or sometimes leave before you get up)? Do they bring work home with them? Do they sometimes work on the weekends?

Do they always have their phone on them in case of an urgent call or email from work? Do they have more than one job? Do they like their job, or do they stay at a job they dislike so they can pay the bills? Do they ever complain about their job? Do they complain about it all the time?

In fact, studies show that most Americans are unhappy with their current job. It's fair to say most Americans would love to be able to opt out and replace their job with something more meaningful and rewarding, even if that something pays a lot less. The unfortunate truth is that the "9-to-5 until you're 65" grind is soul crushing for many.

I have a salaried job as a high school business teacher. I also average much more than forty hours a week (probably close to sixty). When I do the math, my annual salary doesn't look nearly as good as if I worked only forty hours per week. Luckily, I did the math years ago and was okay with the numbers because I love my job, my coworkers, my students, and my school.

What if your future job is *not* like this? What if you dislike, or even hate, your job? Doing something you dislike or hate for five (or more) days a week can be devastating to your happiness.

Getting to FI early in life ensures that whatever, if any, job you will work—and for how many hours per week—is *your* choice.

Why Do People Stay at a Job if They Don't Like It?

There are two common reasons people get trapped in their jobs even though they are unhappy. Let's look at Ben and Tamirah to examine why.

Trap No. 1 Ben took a job that seemed to pay well, only to find out that the number of hours required to perform the job was far more than the forty per week he expected. It happened over time; his average hours per week slowly increased until he realized he was working twelve-hour days. Ben doesn't want to quit his job because he's only had it for a year, and it would look bad to future employers if he switched jobs so soon. Plus, if he did leave, he would lose any sick time and vacation time he's accrued, and his current boss might not give him a good reference. He's also a little scared to start all over at a new job. Filling out all those applications, updating his résumé, finding his suit and tie, brushing up on his interview skills, and taking more tests (drug screenings, skills tests, etc.) doesn't appeal to him at all. Ben has decided to stay put even though he's putting in long hours because it's just less complicated and less risky than leaving. *Trapped.*

Trap No. 2 Tamirah is like most Americans—she spends basically everything she earns. Her monthly paycheck is approximately $3,000, and she usually spends close to or even more than $3,000 each month. Because of that, Tamirah has no savings, which means she is living paycheck to paycheck. She needs that $3,000 each month to pay rent, buy food, make her car payment, and so on. If she were to quit her job and start a new one, the risks would be significant. What if she has one lined up, but it falls through, or she doesn't like it as much as she hoped? What if the new boss decides there is only a part-time position and not a full-time job? Too risky. The only option Tamirah has is to stay put to keep those paychecks coming in so she can pay her bills. *Trapped.*

LIVING FROM PAYCHECK TO PAYCHECK: Being unable to pay your monthly bills if you stop receiving a regular paycheck.

The Bright Side
There *can* be many pluses to a job, however.
- If you do like your coworkers, then the social interactions are fun. (But when you reach FI, you can socialize with whomever you want, whenever you want.)
- Jobs can provide financial security through paychecks, retirement accounts, stock options, and the like. (But when you reach FI, you have, by definition, achieved financial security *without* a job.)

RETIREMENT ACCOUNT: A financial account with favorable tax treatment for holding and growing money until typical retirement age.

- Jobs can give you paid time off, sick pay, and vacation days. (Of course—you guessed it—when you reach FI, every day can be a day off if you wish.)
- Jobs can offer an avenue for furthering your education and challenging yourself mentally. (But, once again, when you reach FI, you can spend your time taking courses and adding to your knowledge however you choose.)
- Jobs can provide health insurance at a very low cost, sometimes free. (Health insurance is a hot topic in our country and its future is extremely uncertain. Once you reach FI, you'll have other options for obtaining low-cost health insurance. If you decide that keeping your job for the health insurance benefit is worthwhile, then do it. However, staying at a job is much more enjoyable when you know you could quit at any time if you wanted.)

The point here is that a job *can* have many upsides. But all those benefits are equally available to you, if not more so, when you are financially independent.

And remember, if you do indeed love your job, you can choose to continue working after reaching FI. Being financially independent means you have several options available, and *you* hold all the cards.

CHAPTER 3:
THE FI EQUATION AND THE FOUR MECHANISMS OF EARLY FI

Live like no one else now, so you can live like no one else later.

—DAVE RAMSEY

@DAVERAMSEY ▶ THE RAMSEY SHOW HIGHLIGHTS

Anything worth having in life comes at a price. To reach a goal or achieve success, you'll have to "pay" with hard work. Dave Ramsey's quote is one of my favorites because it acknowledges that great accomplishments are possible only with some costs.

When you "live like no one else now," you're grinding. You are working hard while most others are watching Netflix, sleeping in, or scrolling aimlessly on social media accounts. When you "live like no one else later," you'll be reaping the rewards of the hard work you put in early on. You'll be in a position of power and control while others will still be clocking in and out of work for decades to come.

If you genuinely desire freedom of time for much of your life, you will need to do things differently than most of your peers over the next few years. But keep in mind that you will only be doing this for the next few *years* in order to enjoy financial independence for five or six *decades*. In my opinion, that's not a bad trade-off.

 FINANCIAL INDEPENDENCE, OR FI: The point at which your *passive income* plus *sustainable asset withdrawal* is greater than your *living expenses* so you no longer have to work for money—also referred to as "financial freedom."

Passive income: Income you earn when not actively working.
Asset withdrawal: Taking money or value out of an existing asset.
Living expenses: All the costs of day-to-day life, such as housing, food, transportation, healthcare, entertainment, and insurance.

The FI Equation

Passive Income + Sustainable Asset Withdrawal > Living Expenses

This simple formula says that you reach FI when your passive income plus your sustainable asset withdrawal is greater than the expenses needed to fund your lifestyle. That sounds pretty straightforward, but it is not always easy to understand.

You probably get what "living expenses" means, but "passive income" and "sustainable asset withdrawal" are more complicated concepts. We'll discuss passive income and asset withdrawal in detail later. For now, I'd like to give you a basic example of each concept to help you understand the FI Equation.

Passive Income:

Imagine you own a house, but instead of living in it, you rent it out to someone else. The person you rent the house to (your tenant) pays you rent each month. The rental income you receive from your tenant more than covers all the expenses of owning the house. After you've paid all those expenses, you have $200 left over each month. This is passive income.

The income is "passive" because you are earning money from this rental house 24/7, no matter what you're doing—whether you're in class, at your job, on a bike ride, or even sleeping.

Sustainable Asset Withdrawal:

If you have $10,000 in a checking account (the asset) and take $100 out, you have made an asset withdrawal. "Sustainable" asset withdrawal occurs when you can make *regular* withdrawals without depleting the asset for a given period of time. For the checking account above (with a balance of $10,000), if you take out $100 each month, that is sustainable for one hundred months, at which time you will have emptied the asset.

It's okay if the FI Equation isn't entirely clear just yet. I wanted to introduce the equation now to lay a foundation for the concepts we will be exploring throughout this book. As you continue reading, you'll understand the FI Equation much better.

The Four Mechanisms of Early FI

To get to the point where you can satisfy the FI Equation, you will be hammering the Four Mechanisms of Early FI. These are *vital* to reaching FI early in life. They each play an essential role in your journey. They are so crucial that Parts Four and Five of this book are dedicated entirely to these critical concepts. For now, let me simply introduce you to the life-changing Four Mechanisms of Early FI. They are:

1. Earn more.
2. Spend less.
3. Save the difference.
4. Invest your savings wisely.

Here's a Look at How Ethan Can Employ Each Mechanism.

- Mechanism 1 involves increasing his income. Ethan could ask his boss for a raise or a promotion, find a better-paying job, work a second job, start a side hustle, or start a small business.
- Mechanism 2 is as simple as it sounds; it means Ethan should spend less than the average person who is in a similar situation. Much less. It means Ethan will *not* spend all the income he receives, even though many Americans do just that.
- Mechanism 3 refers to putting away the difference between what he earns and what he spends. If Ethan earns $1,000 and spends $500, he can save $500 in a savings account. Not too complicated.

- Mechanism 4 involves taking the money he has saved and putting it to work in a smart investment. Let's suppose Ethan has put away $5,000 in a savings account over the last year, and he's ready to invest that money. What should he do with it? That's a great question that we'll tackle later in the book.

Possessions vs. Time

Now that you understand the basics of FI, let's look at it from a higher-level perspective.

Many people think of FI as the ability to buy lots of material possessions. And while FI *can* allow you to buy fancy things, that's not its primary benefit.

In fact, at times FI means pretty much the opposite. If you aspire to own Porsches, mansions, and expensive jewelry, then the version of FI outlined in this book is not what you seek. This book's version of FI will allow you to be comfortable and happy while spending lavishly on the things you *value*, not on things you acquire to impress other people.

Remember the fundamental benefit we discussed in Chapter One? Early FI isn't about the ability to purchase extravagant things. It's about the freedom to enjoy your most precious resource: your *time*.

Ask yourself this question: What do you enjoy doing?

Is it spending time with your friends? Traveling? Going to the beach or the mountains? Playing music or basketball? Spending the day with your family?

No matter what you enjoy doing, you need the *time* to do it. This is why time is more valuable than possessions.

A Personal Example of the Benefits of FI

Skiing was always one of my favorite hobbies, especially when I was younger. I loved spending the day on the mountain, enjoying nature, and pushing myself physically. I loved it so much that in my twenties, I spent two winters working at two different ski resorts: Killington, in Vermont; and Sun Valley, in Idaho.

At age 26, I decided to make Colorado my permanent home. I chose Colorado for many reasons, one of which was to be close to fantastic ski resorts. My ski buddies and I had a saying: "There are no friends on a powder day." This meant that on those rare days with fresh snow and epic skiing, we would go our own way. We each wanted to be selfish to maximize the gift of a powder day. We didn't ride the lift together. We didn't eat lunch together (or more likely, we didn't eat lunch at all). We didn't wait for someone to use the restroom. We didn't ski a run we didn't like because our buddy wanted to. No, a powder day was precious, exciting, and valuable. We had no friends until the lifts closed and it was time to meet back up and talk about our incredible day.

At the time, I was a full-time high school teacher in Denver, working Monday through Friday. Missing a day of work was rare, so the weekends were the days for skiing. I was one of the weekend warriors who would drive from the city to the mountains on Friday evening or early Saturday morning to ski for two glorious days, then drive back on Sunday evening to start the cycle all over again.

Unfortunately, there were *thousands* of us. We all packed into our cars at roughly the same time, resulting in mind-numbing traffic that would add an extra hour to our commute to the ski hill. We all stood in the same long lift lines for anywhere from fifteen to forty-five minutes per run. We all headed into the lodge to buy lunch and hot cocoa at the same time, and we all needed lodging for the same night (Saturday) and paid a premium to the hotels. It was worth it, but barely.

If I had been financially independent at that time, the whole weekend warrior thing would have been irrelevant. If I didn't *have* to work, I would have skied during the week, not on weekends with everybody else. No traffic. No lift lines. Near-empty cafeterias come lunchtime. Plenty of fresh snow on those powder days for me and the other lucky ones out there. Cheap midweek lodging rates instead of sky-high weekend rates. In other words, heaven in the mountains!

But I had not reached FI by 27, or 30, or 35. I was trapped in the weekend warrior mob driving up together, skiing together, and driving back down together in a mad rush to get back for work on Monday morning.

If you start now and reach FI early in life, you will become rich with time. You can then ski or write or practice the guitar or spend time with your friends on a Tuesday or a Friday or any other day you wish. Freedom of time is a beautiful gift that gives you numerous options!

Is the FIRE Movement for You?

Let's go back to the survey I gave my students, because I asked them one more question: "How would your life change (for better or worse) if you were financially independent (didn't have to work) by age 30?"

Answer that question in your head right now. Take a minute to think about your answer, then continue.

Now that you have *your* answer, let's look at some of my students' responses. Keep in mind, I did not prep my students in any way—I had not taught or even discussed anything about personal finance, investing, or FI at the time I gave this survey.

A few students said that early FI would not be ideal for them:

- "I wouldn't have a purpose. I feel that in today's society, working (especially if you enjoy your work—which you should) gives people direction and daily goals that are crucial to mental health and happiness."
- "I would probably have a lot less stress in my life, but I also might be really bored and not know what to do with my time."
- "I would have too much free time and would not know what to do with myself."

These responses show that early FI is not for everyone. Some people would prefer to follow the tried-and-true version of the American Dream and work for the better part of their life. As I've said before, there is nothing wrong with that. If the responses above resemble your own answer, then this book and early FI may not be for you.

These students' responses could also indicate a misunderstanding that FI is the same as retirement. As we discussed earlier, with FI you *can* keep working to give yourself purpose and avoid boredom.

Many of my students said they would continue to work or do other work they would enjoy. They wrote things like:

- "I would still work to save but also choose a career that I would truly love."
- "It wouldn't really change. I don't really spend that much money, and I really enjoy working on what I am passionate about. I highly doubt I would stop working. I would just be able to give more to the institutions I care about."
- "If I didn't have to work after the age of 30, I would still work anyway. I feel that it is an obligation to consistently be making

money while I am able to do so because that way my kids or family will be even better off. Hopefully, I would be able to continue doing whatever it was that led to me being that fiscally successful by age 30."

These students saw the value of being financially independent and understood that early FI offers the option of working how and when you want.

Finally, most of the students thought being financially independent would be beneficial:

- "My life would be better if I was financially stable because I could go out into the world and do things that I always wanted to do."
- "I would continue to live my life but also become closer with my family and friends and realize all the things I didn't see in life while I was too busy working."
- "I would have time to travel and learn new things and meet new people rather than having to work every day."
- "I would have more time to do the things I love, like hiking, snowboarding, and fishing."
- "My life would be better without the worry of money. I would probably do more community service or nonprofit work."
- "My happiness level would go way up, and I would live a more full life."
- "You would have the opportunity to pursue things you are more interested in or passionate about, rather than having to do something you are not passionate about because you need to earn a living."
- "You would have such a dope life—being able to do what you want and really be able to explore the world and see everything."

The purpose of this book is to provide you with options. Up until now, most young people were only aware of one option—the typical approach to the American Dream. But the FIRE movement provides other, lesser-known options that are only now starting to come to light.

The FIRE movement and its strategies are here if you need them. It's your choice. Do what you think is best for you. But, at the very least, you should read the rest of this book so you are fully informed about the early FI option. Then you can make the best decision for your future.

The Journey Ahead

If you asked one hundred people if they would like to be in great physical shape, almost everyone would say yes. We all know what we need to do to be in fantastic shape: work out daily and eat healthy foods. It's not a mystery. It's actually very simple. So why isn't everyone in the best shape of their lives? Well, because it's not *easy*.

Achieving FI at a very early age is no different. It's not complicated; this book and hundreds of other resources are available to those who would like to reach FI early in life, yet few ever get there. That's because it's not easy. It's one thing to *know* how to do something—*doing* it is entirely different.

Not everyone will have enough motivation and determination to do the work required to reach early FI. Many more will lose enthusiasm because they can't grasp the enormous value of reaching FI decades before turning 65. They'll struggle to comprehend how those years of freedom can completely change their life for the better. Others will simply not have the courage to take a very different path from their parents, peers, and friends.

If you want to achieve early FI, you must accept that you will be making certain sacrifices along the way. You must also be focused on the end reward: freedom of time. Many people have done it before you, as you will see from the Featured Freak case studies in this book. It is entirely possible as long as you're up for the challenge.

If you are feeling fearful because the ideas of early FI, frugality, passive income, and investing seem too daunting or confusing, that's okay. It's not unusual to feel that way when considering something new. Let me give you an example of a very similar fear I see in my students every year.

The students in my classes compete in a business club called DECA. The competitions consist of doing business role-plays with adult judges. Further, as if that isn't scary enough, the students don't know the |exact situation they will be role-playing until just a few minutes before they compete.

During the first week of school in August, I tell my students that the first DECA competition will be in November.

I can see the fear and anxiety build in my students' eyes (they often verbalize it too) as they imagine themselves doing these role-plays in front of an adult judge. I quickly remind them that they will not be doing these competitive role-plays tomorrow or next week or even that month—

they will be learning, practicing, and polishing their skills in class until they are fully confident and prepared. I tell them it's my job to push them beyond their comfort zone, but it's also my job to prepare them for their new endeavor so they succeed.

Then, when the time comes every year for our first competition, the students finish their role-plays and say things like, "That was not as bad as I thought it would be," or "Wow, I think I did really well!" I've even heard, "That was actually kind of fun!"

When it comes to early FI, you're in a similar situation. The concepts may seem overwhelming and difficult, but remember, you don't just have *months* to get ready, you have *years*! And the job of this book is to prepare you and build your confidence so when the day comes to start implementing these strategies, you are not only ready, you actually have fun doing it.

Most people, especially young people like yourself, are *never* exposed to the information contained in this book. *Ever.* Whatever you can take away from this book will put you miles ahead of others and well on your way to becoming a FI Freak!

If you are unsure whether you have what it takes for this journey, please finish this book before deciding. We will be diving into some powerful topics to help you realize if you have the right stuff to be a true FI Freak. For what it's worth, I sincerely hope that you do.

RACHEL RICHARDS

@ @moneyhoneyrachel

♪ @moneyhoneyrachel

Where do you currently live?
Colorado Springs, Colorado.

How old are you?
Twenty-eight.

How old were you when you started actively pursuing financial independence?
Twenty-four.

What was your profession/career/job when you first started pursuing FI?
Financial advisor.

Do you consider yourself financially independent today?
Yes.

If you have reached FI, how many years did it take you to get there?
Two and a half years.

If you have reached FI, what profession/career/job do you have now, if any?
I quit my full-time job in 2019 and now live off more than $15,000 per month in passive income. My biggest income streams are my rental properties and royalty income from my books, but my husband and I have five to six passive income streams total.

Who or what got you started on your FI path?
I read the book *Rich Dad Poor Dad* in high school and always knew I wanted to invest in real estate. On a deeper note, I grew up in a wealthy county and my parents didn't manage their finances well. We were always short on money and couldn't do things as a family. I felt like I didn't fit in, which is not how you want to feel in middle school or high school. I wanted to grow up and be different from everyone struggling with money. I wanted to be able to take care of myself and my loved ones.

What is your Why of FI?

I grew up inheriting a lot of limiting beliefs and fears around money. My biggest fear is not having enough money to take care of myself or my loved ones. That fear has been a large motivating factor for me.

What are your plans for the future?

Now that I've reached FI, my why is about continuing to make an impact. I can help other women and young people learn about and achieve FI as well. I enjoy the freedom to work when, where, and if I want. And I have the time to travel the country and world, and to hike all the mountains.

What is or has been your favorite way to save money and why?

My favorite way is to focus on *increasing income*! Too often we get caught up in cutting costs and sacrificing/giving something up in order to save more money. I prefer just making more money to cover an expense.

What is your current savings rate?

My husband and I have a savings rate of anywhere from 30 to 40 percent.

If you invest in the stock market, what is your preferred type of investment or method?

Index funds.

How many real estate properties do you own? What types are they?

My husband and I own six buildings, thirty-eight units total: two single-family homes, one duplex, and three buildings that are ten to twelve units each.

What has been your biggest challenge in pursing FI and why?

Limiting beliefs and fears. The fear of not knowing enough. The fear of not having enough money or losing money on an investment. The fear of making a mistake. The fear that I'm not good enough. All of these fears have held me back at one point or another. And even though I achieved FI at age 27, I probably could have done it sooner if I hadn't doubted myself so much.

Would you change anything about your path to FI? If so, what?

I would have gotten started in real estate investing sooner.

What one piece of advice would you give a teenager who wants to achieve early FI?

Anyone, at any age, on any income, can achieve FI. I'm not a trust fund baby, and I never made six figures from a job. If I can do it in under three years, so can you. My favorite quote is from Zig Ziglar: "You don't have to be great to start, but you have to start to be great."

If, at this point, you are convinced that you are a FI Freak, and you are excited about what you've read so far, then you should be confident and proud of your new standing. And to celebrate that, you should declare to the world that you are a FI Freak and proud of it. Take a photo of yourself with this page open and post it on your social media with the hashtags **#PROUDFREAK** and **#TEENAGEFIFREAK**.

Don't forget to tag **@BIGGERPOCKETS** and **@SHEEKSFREAKS!**

I AM A *Proud* FI FREAK!

PART TWO

THE FI FOUNDATION

Someone with a poor mindset will say, "I can't afford it." Someone with a wealth mindset will say, "How can I afford it?"

—ROBERT KIYOSAKI
@ @THEREALKIYOSAKI ▶ THE RICH DAD CHANNEL

Part Two is all about building a solid foundation for the remaining concepts in this book. In Chapter Four, we'll examine happiness and discover what brings you true joy and contentment. We'll also take a look at how happiness is connected to money but not dependent on it.

The concept of "enough" is the subject of Chapter Five, and Chapter Six will ask you to take a hard look at your motivations by examining your Why of FI.

Finally, Chapter Seven will dive into the four entrepreneurial traits that are crucial for success as you begin to forge ahead on your early FI pathway.

CHAPTER 4:
HAPPINESS

Let's look at how happiness ties into early FI. Take five minutes to make a list of the top ten things that bring you happiness, in no particular order. These could be activities, people, possessions, events, hobbies, or anything else. Write your list below.

The Top Ten Things That Make Me Happy

1. _____

2. _____

3. _____

4. _____

5. _____

6. _____

7. _____

8. _____

9. _____

10. _____

If you didn't create a list, go back and do it now! For this chapter to be meaningful, you must complete your happiness list.

Can Money Buy Happiness?

Spending money is not linked to happiness.

—MR. AND MRS. PLANTING OUR PENNIES,
BIGGERPOCKETS MONEY PODCAST, EPISODE 32

If being happy is one of your highest priorities in life (as I assume it is for most people), you should focus on the things you wrote down on your happiness list. Unfortunately, most people fall into the trap of thinking that more money will bring more happiness. That's simply not true.

Don't believe it? Look at your list again. Take a minute and circle all your answers that are free or very low cost.

Chances are you circled many of the items on your list. The circled items are not things money can buy. They are instead based on qualities like fulfillment, gratification, being of service, and love. For example, I'll bet "spending time with my friends" made it onto your list. Thankfully, it doesn't cost much money to spend time with your friends if you're hanging out in a park, watching your favorite show, going for a walk, or FaceTiming.

Isn't it amazing how many things that bring us happiness cost very little, yet people spend so much of their precious time working to make more and more money? You don't have to be filthy rich to be happy. Everything you circled on your list proves that.

This is extremely important: FI is not about having lots of *money*. It's about having lots of *time* to enjoy the items on your happiness list.

Hedonic Adaptation

Most folks are about as happy as they make up their minds to be.

—ATTRIBUTED TO ABRAHAM LINCOLN

One concept that illustrates how more money will not bring more happiness is hedonic adaptation. This idea dates back centuries. It refers to our tendency to return to a reasonably steady level of happiness after any negative or positive event in our life. According to hedonic adaptation, we all have a happiness set point, which is the average amount of happiness you feel day in and day out. The idea is that whether you experience a terrible or a wonderful event in your life, you will automatically return to your happiness set point after a period of time.

FREAK SPEAK

HEDONIC ADAPTATION: The tendency to return to a baseline level of happiness despite major positive or negative events or life changes.

For example, let's say you are a reasonably happy person. We'll even put a number on it: On the happiness scale, you average 8 out of 10. But then you get an email from a prospective college. And not just *any* college—your number one choice. This is the college you have been dreaming of attending for years. It has the perfect campus and the perfect program for your career goals at the perfect distance from home. Attending this college means *everything* to you.

The email says, "We regret to inform you . . ."

You were not accepted. You're not even on the waitlist.

You are devastated. It's impossible to imagine going anywhere but *that* college. So much for getting your dream job—other schools' programs pale in comparison. Your happiness level just dropped to a big fat 1. Life sucks.

Hedonic adaptation tells us that eventually you'll be an 8 again. Flash-forward one month from your hypothetical college rejection. At this point, you've gotten past the disappointment and negative thoughts. Instead, you've become excited about attending a different school to meet amazing new friends and start enjoying the next phase of your life. You are back to your happiness set point of 8.

Of course, the severity of any given life event will change how long it takes to get back to your happiness set point. You might bounce back from a fender bender in a couple of days. However, if someone very close to you dies, you might need a few months to find your 8 again. But eventually, you will return to that happiness set point.

This same concept applies to money. If you were to inherit $1000 from a distant relative, you would undoubtedly be at 10 for a while. On the other hand, if you lost a high-paying job and wound up in financial turmoil, you might dip to a 3. Either way, after some time, you'd be back to 8 in no time. In other words, money in and of itself won't change your happiness level, at least not for long.

Genuinely increasing your baseline of happiness requires a change in mindset. Happiness is related to how you approach the world—it's not something you will achieve after you have more money or achieve a particular life goal.

How to Aim High

In 2015, a young man named Laurence Lewars gave a fascinating TED Talk titled "Questions Every Teenager Needs to Be Asked." (I highly encourage you to watch the YouTube video. It's only eighteen minutes long.)

Laurence surveyed hundreds of teens from diverse backgrounds and asked two main questions.

The first was, "What do you see yourself doing in fifteen years?"

(Take a couple of minutes and think about your answer to this question. Yes, you!)

Then he asked, "What would you be doing in fifteen years if you could do absolutely anything?"

(Answer this question for yourself as well. Do it now.)

Your answer to the first question was probably something like "Working as an engineer, living in Chicago, married, with one or two kids." You may have picked a different job or location, but the basic idea was likely similar.

These answers tend to be greatly influenced by *outside* factors. For example, maybe your dad or mom sees you as a lawyer because they are lawyers themselves. Or maybe the messages you've received from society (social media, teachers, mentors, books, friends) have told you that going to college and being a scientist, or architect, or police officer is best for you. Your answer was probably a mashup of many outside influences and your own goals.

With the second question, however, Laurence eliminated those outside influences by getting teens to think only of what *they* wanted. He stripped away the input from parents, friends, social media, and society, leaving behind only *their* personal vision.

What do *you* dream about doing fifteen years from now? Maybe you'd like to own a surf shop on a beach or be a stay-at-home parent. Whatever your response—and everybody's is unique—chances are it was very different from your answer to the first one, and you are not alone. Laurence found that 78 percent of the teens he surveyed changed their answers as well.

Why did so many teens have different responses? Laurence thinks that teens are giving up on their dreams due to outside influences. Maybe it's because of their parents' expectations. Maybe it's because of society's beliefs. Another possibility is that they want to be financially secure, and their "dream" answer usually doesn't allow them to earn enough money to have that financial security. If you dream of owning a surf shop, how would you afford to get it started? That's a tough one. The backup option (your answer to the first question) is the more rational, and so most people focus on that option instead.

Laurence says, "We're living in a world where dreams take a back seat to job security." Job security provides safety: financially, emotionally, and socially. There's nothing wrong with these things—except that in exchange we have to give up on our dreams, and that's a huge sacrifice!

Teens are taught to follow the traditional American Dream pathway we discussed in Chapter Two. Dreams don't fit into this "practical" path unless the dream happens to include a high-paying job, so what you are genuinely passionate about gets pushed aside until later in life. Once retired at age 65, you can *then* revisit your dreams because you now have the time and money to pursue them—but only if those dreams are still realistic. (E.g., Can you be a stay-at-home parent at 65?)

In his presentation, Laurence mentions one of my favorite quotes from Les Brown: "Most people fail in life, not because they aim too high and miss, but because they aim too low and hit." What if you could aim high (reach for your dreams and passions) while you are young *and* have financial security while doing so?

By reaching FI early in life, you'll be free to pursue your dreams and passions because you'll be financially secure decades before most people. This will prevent you from aiming low and hitting, and it will bring you more happiness because you'll be doing what you want to do.

Why Are We Even Talking About Happiness?

While it is safe to say that money isn't necessarily a source of happiness, those who build wealth and attain financial freedom generally have more choices in life and more opportunities to seek that happiness than those who do not.

—SCOTT TRENCH, *SET FOR LIFE*
@SCOTT_TRENCH

If you, like most people, believe life's highest goal is to be happy, don't get caught up in the race for the best car, the biggest house, the most lavish vacations, or the most followers on social media. Instead, pay attention to the things you put on your happiness list. And know that early FI will give you more freedom of time to enjoy them.

CHAPTER 5:
THE CONCEPT OF ENOUGH

Financial Independence has nothing to do with [being] rich. It is the experience of having enough.

—VICKI ROBIN AND JOE DOMINGUEZ, *YOUR MONEY OR YOUR LIFE*
:camera: @VICKIROBIN

As we've seen, the items on our happiness list—most of which have nothing to do with money—are the key to enjoying life. That's not to say that money and possessions can't add to our overall happiness. But beyond a certain point they can actually take happiness away. When it comes to money and possessions, what we need in order to be happy is simply to have "enough."

The Happiness Curve

In *Your Money or Your Life,* Vicki Robin and Joe Dominguez use something they call "the fulfillment curve"—which I prefer to call "the happiness curve"—to illustrate the concept of "enough."

The Fulfillment Curve: Enough

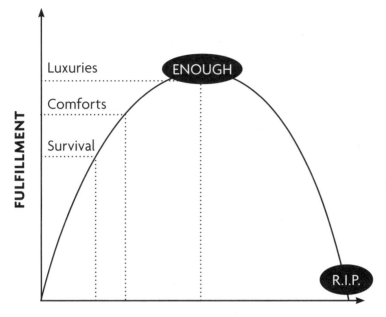

This curve shows the relationship between our happiness (fulfillment) and the amount of money we spend. As we first spend money to meet our basic survival needs, our happiness begins. Then, as we continue to spend money on additional comforts and luxuries, our happiness increases. But there comes a point at which spending additional money does *not* add to our happiness. Beyond the point of "enough" on the chart, our happiness actually *decreases* as we spend more.

The "survival" point indicates when our basic needs—such as shelter, food, and clothing—are met. (When I speak of food and clothing here, I'm not talking about high-end items. The clothing doesn't *have* to be brand-name, and the food doesn't *have* to be gourmet. Those are luxuries, not necessities.) If we don't meet these basic needs, we will not experience happiness because we are concerned only with survival and safety.

However, it *is* okay to spend money on more than the bare minimum. We all deserve to splurge and treat ourselves occasionally. My wife and I went on a cruise recently. I would definitely consider a cruise a luxury item, but it was a trip we valued and had saved up for. These purchases are part of living a fulfilled life, and we should not feel guilty about them. These extra items will add even more happiness to our lives, up to the point of enough.

Enough is the point at which your happiness is maximized. You have everything you need plus a little extra. You are not stressing about making ends meet, but you are not weighed down with possessions or debt either.

If you continue to spend money to acquire things beyond this point, you will not increase your happiness. Any more spending will lead to more worry, commitments, and obligations. For example, buying a boat can bring joy to your family in the future. But it also comes with the stress of regular maintenance, annual registration fees, insurance payments, storage requirements, as well as the fear of breakdowns, accidents, and loss to theft. The amount of happiness a boat can contribute to your life depends on where you're at on your happiness curve.

The important people in our lives bring us more happiness than our possessions. We know this. We smile and laugh more when we are with our best friend than when we are in a closet full of designer clothes. Clothes can't make us laugh so hard our face hurts. Neither can an exquisite downtown loft or a $100 steak dinner. We could eat peanut butter and jelly sandwiches in the park with our friends and have a fantastic time.

The trick is not to fall into the trap of thinking that you *need* lots of stuff to be happy. You are smarter than that. You are beginning to understand that enough, combined with the amazing people in your life, is all you need for abundant happiness.

The Common Misconception

Many people who are not familiar with the concept of early FI believe it means a life of luxury and lavish spending. These people are focused on acquiring things like an extravagant house, a high-end car, designer clothes, and exotic vacations.

On your journey to early FI, you'll be tempted by this common misconception. You will need to ask yourself, "Which is more important to me—more possessions or more freedom?"

This is the choice you'll make every time you consider making a purchase. If you choose to acquire more stuff, you are prolonging the length of time it will take you to reach FI. That means you are decreasing the amount of free time in your future. If you determine, after careful consideration, that making a certain purchase will add enough happiness to your life to offset the additional time needed to achieve FI, then go for it.

Whenever you consider a big purchase, weigh the added happiness against the additional time needed to reach FI. For example, suppose you were considering a one-week trip to Hawaii that would cost $3,000. You could also choose to invest that $3,000 instead. If it were to earn a 7 percent return over the next fifteen years, that investment would be worth just over $8,000. If, at that time, your annual expenses were $48,000, then that $8,000 would cover two months of expenses. So, when deciding on the trip, you should ask yourself which is more valuable to you: the week in Hawaii, or reaching FI two months earlier. There is no right answer, but asking the question is the Freakish thing to do!

Many studies indicate that once a person reaches a certain income level, their happiness doesn't necessarily increase. This is the level of income that provides enough. It allows you to be safe in a modest home with food and clothing to meet your needs and money left over for fun, investing, and a few luxury purchases.

For most people, this amount seems to be around $40,000 to $50,000 a year; for a couple, it's $70,000 to $80,000 a year. (These amounts may vary based on the cost of living in different areas.) Once they go past that "enough" income level, the happiness curve tells us their happiness is more likely to decrease than increase.

Vicki Robin and Joe Dominguez would often give seminars about the idea of enough. What they found illustrates how easily we can fall victim to the misconception that more income will make us happier:

> In our early seminars in the 1980s, we'd collect data from participants and analyze it on the spot to reflect the audience back to itself . . . [When asked], "[H]ow much would it take to make you happy?" almost everyone, in every income bracket, said: "50 percent more than I have now." When asked to rate their happiness on a scale of 1 to 5, there was no significant difference between the top and bottom earners. You could hear a pin drop as people realized that the person in the row ahead of them probably had the "more" they thought would make them happy—and it made no difference.

A Generous Example of Enough

Julia Wise and Jeff Kaufman, a couple in their late twenties, were living their normal lives in Massachusetts. Julia was a social worker, and Jeff was a computer programmer. They felt they had everything they needed and were more interested in giving back than spending more, so they decided to live on "enough" for a year. Their combined income was slightly less than $250,000, but they went through the entire year spending money only on their enough. How much did that cost? About $20,000. They also invested around $78,000 for their future and retirement. Including the $54,000 they paid in taxes, this came to a bit more than $150,000. This means they had an extra $100,000 beyond what they needed.

What did they do with their extra income? They donated it! Yes, Julia and Jeff donated about $100,000 in one year. They realized the extra money wasn't going to make them any happier, so why not give it to someone who truly needed it?

The couple has done this for many years now. And guess what? They are very happy—probably happier than most because they have the pleasure of knowing they've donated more than half a million dollars to help others. Kudos to them!

Some Final Words on Enough

If the lifestyle you envision doesn't currently align with the enough model and your goal is to earn as much money as possible to buy *whatever* you want, that's okay. When I was young, that was my primary motivation too.

However, as you read this book, your perception may change. We all come to understand what *really* makes us happy in our own time. It took me a couple of decades. I hope your realization comes much faster. Wherever you are today with the concept of enough, you can still move forward on a path to early FI where happiness will be much easier to obtain, no matter your goals.

CHAPTER 6:
YOUR WHY OF FI

What holds most people back is bravery. Now, you can try to be braver just by willing yourself to do it, but that's not going to work for most people. What does work for people is having a very big "why." What matters to you? What drives you? What are your goals? What is propelling you? What is motivating you? They are all [questions] that are describing the thing that's going to push you through whatever your fears, your excuses, or your concerns really are. So… ask yourself, "What is my why? What motivates me? What drives me? And is it worth getting over the excuses that I have to stop me from taking action?"

—DAVID GREENE, *THE BIGGERPOCKETS PODCAST*, EPISODE 336
@DAVIDGREENE24   DAVID GREENE REAL ESTATE

Know Your "Why"

It's time to think about some important questions: Why are you reading this book? Why are you considering working toward early financial independence? What is your real motivation? What is your underlying inspiration for your upcoming FI journey? These are critical questions, so take some time right now to think about them.

What was the first thought that came into your head when you considered these questions? What was the second? The third? Start a note in your phone or a Google Doc and title it "My Why of FI." Type out your answers so you can look at them often and update them as they change over time (and they will).

There shouldn't be only *one* reason. You will likely have two, three, or four, and when you add up all your reasons, you get your Why of FI. Your Why of FI is the totality of your motivations and inspirations. It's what led you to research early FI, and keeping it in mind is essential to your success.

FREAK
SPEAK

WHY OF FI: The totality of your motivations and inspirations for pursuing early financial independence.

The path to early FI is not easy. You will have to make some sacrifices. There will be several speed bumps, roadblocks, and detours along the way—times when nothing appears to be going right and the universe seems to be plotting against you.

When times get tough, looking at your Why of FI list will restore your motivation. It will remind you of the reasons you began this endeavor in the first place. Without your Why of FI list, it is far more likely that your journey will stall. You may even give up and go back to a non–FI Freak life.

Some of your reasons for pursuing early FI are probably simple and self-focused. Other reasons are bigger-picture or rooted in a desire to help others. I call the first category the "lower-level whys" and the second the "higher-level whys."

Lower-Level Whys

Whether you want early financial freedom so you can focus on raising a family, pursuing a hobby, relaxing on the beach, traveling the world, or making an impact on your community, the reason you're working toward early financial freedom needs to be at the forefront.

—SCOTT TRENCH, *SET FOR LIFE*
@SCOTT_TRENCH

The most common reason for pursuing early FI boils down to one word: time. Time is your most valuable resource, and it is *not* renewable. You only get so much of it in your life. There are only twenty-four hours in a day, and that will never change.

Our other resources, for the most part, are renewable or replaceable. If we spend $100, we can work to earn another $100. If we wreck our car, we can get a new one. If we lose a job, we can apply for a different position. But we cannot get back *any* of our time. Once we spend it, it's gone forever. (Kind of makes you rethink all those hours you've spent surfing YouTube, huh?)

The freedom of time is one reason for pursuing FI. Some other popular reasons include:

- Having the freedom to explore all opportunities in your life
- Not having a boss or someone else telling you what to do for the next forty-five years
- Having more fun in your life and not working sixty hours a week
- Having the freedom to start your own business and be an entrepreneur

These are all lower-level reasons. As I mentioned before, they are more simple and self-focused. There's nothing wrong with any of these—they are what initially piques our interest and, at times, keeps us focused on our end goal. Do any of the reasons listed above resonate with your motivation?

Go back to your Why of FI list and create a subsection called "My Lower-Level Whys." Move any appropriate whys under this heading. Don't write anything down just because you think it sounds good—only include things that mean something to you. If you have only one or two, that's okay.

Higher-Level Whys

The significance of you will remain forever obscure to you, but you may assume you are fulfilling your significance and are getting close to your life's purpose if you devote your time and attention to converting all your experience to the highest advantage of others.

—R. BUCKMINSTER FULLER, *IDEAS AND INTEGRITIES*

Many people think of FI as an opportunity to sit on a tropical beach sipping on Mai Tais and watching the sun set over the ocean waves, then heading back up to their hotel suite to get ready for a gourmet dinner. Although this can absolutely be a part of your early FI picture, it won't satisfy your inner need to contribute and grow. There are other, more generous uses of our time that can bring us satisfaction and a higher sense of gratitude.

Higher-level whys are less self-based and are more focused on helping others. In fact, these reasons pack a much bigger punch when it comes to fueling a long-lasting motivation for your journey ahead—and they can't be faked.

Hopefully, when you wrote down your Why of FI list, you had one or two reasons that fell into this category. If not, I challenge you to come up with at least one higher-level why. It's important to find an external purpose that you feel passionate about. Otherwise, if you are heading down this road only for your own self-interest, you probably will never achieve your goal.

By helping others, we also help ourselves. Various studies have shown that when we serve others, we increase our own happiness. Your higher-level why could benefit the greater good *and* increase your well-being at the same time.

When you reach early FI, you will be blessed with the gift of time. You can make the most of that time by choosing to do what fuels your soul. Here are some higher-level goals to get you thinking along those lines:

- Mentoring young people and teaching them what you know about achieving FI
- Starting a nonprofit to provide safe, affordable housing
- Devoting abundant amounts of time to raising your children
- Volunteering at your local museum, library, or neighborhood clean-up
- Donating your time at an animal shelter
- Helping out at a local food bank
- Engaging in political activism for a cause you believe in
- Spending time assisting the disabled, elderly, or terminally ill
- Planting trees, cleaning up hiking trails, or starting a recycling drive in your community
- Helping set up children's shelters in developing countries

Go back to your Why of FI list and create a subsection called "My Higher-Level Whys." Move any appropriate whys under this heading. As before, don't write something down just because you think it sounds good. And if you only have one or two, that's okay.

Take a few more minutes to think about your Why of FI after you finish this chapter. Once you have some clarity, update your list based on your new understanding of your lower- and higher-level whys. Next, put a monthly reminder in your phone or calendar to look at and possibly update your Why of FI list. By committing now to reviewing your list once a month, you are helping your future self get through tough times. You are also increasing the odds you will indeed serve others when the opportunities materialize.

It's been a while since you posted about your journey. Post a video of yourself describing your Why of FI. Or post a picture of yourself with this page and list your Why of FI motives in the caption. Tell the world why you are choosing to make sacrifices in the present for rewards in the future. Don't be shy or embarrassed about your reasons.

Don't forget to use **#MYWHYOFFI** and **#TEENAGEFIFREAK** and to tag **@BIGGERPOCKETS** and **@SHEEKSFREAKS!**

My WHY OF FI

CHAPTER 7:
THE ENTREPRENEURIAL MINDSET

All our dreams can come true, if we have the courage to pursue them.

—WALT DISNEY

Why talk about entrepreneurship in a book about early financial independence? As it turns out, the journey to early FI is very similar to the journey of the entrepreneur. Some might even say we are each the entrepreneur of our own life. We are the boss who makes all the decisions, some good and some bad. We carry all the risk and delight in all the rewards.

By now you know that the path to early FI is for exceptional individuals. These individuals share certain personality traits that have helped them find Freakish success—traits that are also typical of the entrepreneurial mindset. In preparation for your FI journey, you will need to reframe the way you think about rules, knowledge, decisiveness, and failure. This is where the entrepreneurial mindset is key.

Why Doesn't Everyone Jump on Board the FI Train?

On your path to early FI, you will certainly mention your ambitions to your friends and family (as you should). And you'll find that only a few of them will be genuinely curious about the decisions you're making and the strategies you're learning. Even fewer—perhaps only one or two—will ask questions because they are interested in joining you while on their own FI journey.

Why don't our friends and family get it? Why aren't they as excited as we are? Why won't they listen to our reasoning when we are trying to help them see what we see?

Because these people don't possess the traits we will be examining in this chapter—and that's okay. Once again, this journey is not easy and, therefore, not for everyone.

In fact, most people will not understand your desire and motivation for early FI, so be prepared. You will experience negativity from those around you. I'm not suggesting that your friends and family don't want you to succeed—of course that's not true. So why will some of them rain on your FI parade?

The reason is usually that they are trying to justify their decision *not* to pursue FI themselves.

It's all about FOMO. When we succeed, we prove that the FI path is a viable way to quickly grow wealth, or at least quicker than the traditional strategies *they* are using. When it works for us, they may realize they made a mistake by ignoring the opportunity.

There's little to be gained by defending your decisions to these cynics, but understanding their real motivations may help lessen the sting of their disapproval

So, what is it we have that they don't?

The Four Traits That Are Vital for Your FI Journey

1. A Propensity for Breaking the Rules

Know the rules well, so you can break them effectively.

—ATTRIBUTED TO THE DALAI LAMA

In school, teachers give students step-by-step instructions on what to do to get an A. In order to succeed, students have been conditioned to be obedient rule followers. Of course, there are students who often say to me, "Just tell me what to do, and I'll do it."

This approach does not encourage young people to take risks or deviate from the beaten path. To be successful outside of the typical American Dream takes creativity and divergent thinking, not memorization skills or an astonishing ability to follow the rules.

If you're an A student, I'll bet you're pretty smart and a great rule follower. If you're a C or D student, you very well may still be pretty smart but *not* a very good rule follower. Here's the bad (or good) news. To excel at what this book is suggesting, you need to have an entrepreneurial mindset, and that mindset includes a non-rule-following mentality. It could be that a C student will have a better shot at making this whole thing work for them because they are used to doing things their own way. That may not be great for getting As, but it's definitely great for being an entrepreneur.

Steve Jobs (Apple), Mark Zuckerberg (Facebook), Bill Gates (Microsoft), Travis Kalanick (Uber), John Mackey (Whole Foods), and Jack Dorsey (Twitter and Square) all dropped out of college. Following rules was not their strength, but that mentality served them extremely well in their entrepreneurial endeavors.

Now, if you're an A student, don't fret. You may struggle with getting used to doing things your own way at first, but you can still develop an entrepreneurial mindset. Many successful entrepreneurs did finish college, and with excellent grades.

The entrepreneurial mindset is not about staying inside the box. It's not about jumping through all the right hoops, following the status quo, or always being obedient and compliant.

Instead, it's about taking risks and sometimes failing. It's about getting back up when you do fail. It's about putting yourself out there, having a problem-solving mentality, and thinking for yourself. And it's about breaking some rules along the way.

2. An Insatiable Thirst for Knowledge

An investment in knowledge always pays the best interest.

—ATTRIBUTED TO BENJAMIN FRANKLIN

Once we leave high school, additional education is a choice. Many opt to continue their education formally—with a degree or certification—then stop. But an entrepreneur's education never ends, because entrepreneurs never stop learning. For them, the continuous acquisition of knowledge is as necessary as food and oxygen.

Learning is not confined to the classroom. In fact, the vast majority of our learning takes place outside of school. For example, you're reading this book because you've chosen to add to your knowledge in order to improve your future.

There are numerous ways to seek out knowledge. Entrepreneurs use as many of them as possible to constantly satisfy their hunger for information. Here is a short list of ways to gain knowledge beyond school:

- Attend a free or low-cost seminar
- Find a mentor
- Read books
- Listen to podcasts
- Read blogs
- Talk to others
- Watch YouTube videos

We will be using all of these learning methods and more throughout the FI Freak Checklist to satisfy your constant thirst for knowledge.

3. The Ability to Pull the Trigger at the Right Time

Next in importance to having a good aim is to recognize when to pull the trigger.

—DAVID LETTERMAN

You will never know *everything* about reaching early FI, but there will come a time when you will know enough. Will you be able to pull the trigger when that time comes? That's the real test of the entrepreneur.

There exists a spectrum of decision making. One extreme is making decisions without *any* information, and this is the choice of fools. They're quick on the draw and as a result often fall victim to scams and wind up broke without knowing what happened.

At the other extreme are those who always seek *more* information and as a result fail to act. They are the "paralysis by analysis" types who want to have every detail figured out and therefore can never make a decision. They are continually seeking that additional piece of insight or always waiting for the perfect opportunity. Neither ever comes, and in the end, they do nothing.

FREAK SPEAK

PARALYSIS BY ANALYSIS: A perpetual state of indecisiveness because of a constant needless desire to either understand more or gain additional information.

Entrepreneurs can tell when they know enough. Once they are confident in their knowledge, they act. They are able to *know* when they *know* what they need to *know*.

Recognizing when to pull the trigger is critical. If you're unsure about your ability to do this, the FI Freak Checklist in Appendix A will help you understand when you're ready to make key decisions along your journey to FI.

4. Having an Unusually Low Fear of Failure

I've missed more than 9,000 shots in my career. I've lost almost 300 games. Twenty-six times I've been trusted to take the game-winning shot and missed. I've failed over and over and over again in my life. And that is why I succeed.

—MICHAEL JORDAN

Success does not come without failure. Period.

It took Thomas Edison a thousand attempts to come up with a working light bulb. The best-selling author Stephen King racked up thirty rejections for his first book, *Carrie*, before Doubleday agreed to publish it. George Lucas took his idea for *Star Wars* to Disney, United Artists, and Universal and was sent walking each time until Fox finally decided to roll the dice.

Entrepreneurs don't fear failure; they *thrive* on it. They understand that failure is key: It brings education, knowledge, growth, confidence, and opportunity. Failure is about trying, putting yourself out there, defying the norms, exploring outside the box. It's about ignoring the hoops so you can jump through walls. It's about challenging the status quo.

Unfortunately, most people are too concerned about what others will think if they fail, or they're too worried about the consequences of failure. Entrepreneurs, however, are more concerned with the consequences if they *don't* fail. They know that there is no success without risk.

Taking a risk and failing is better than not taking a risk at all. Instead of fearing failure, learn to appreciate what failure can offer you.

MARQUEZ GRIFFIN

@marquez_griffin

Where do you currently live?
Denver, Colorado.

How old are you?
Twenty-five.

How old were you when you started actively pursuing financial independence? Twenty-two.

What was your profession/career/job when you first started pursuing FI?
Sheet metal journeyman.

Do you consider yourself financially independent today? No.

If you have not yet reached FI, at what age do you see yourself getting there? Forty.

Who or what got you started on your FI path?
My friend's dad is financially independent, with more than twenty-five real estate properties that are paid for in full. This was inspiring for me.

What is your Why of FI?
To financially give back to everyone that has helped me in life. To have quality time with my family and friends. To have more time to volunteer with organizations, to build gardens, and to help the Earth.

What are your plans for the future?
I am working on improving my real estate business while also working as a notary signing agent. I intend to write books, make video courses that help improve people's lives, and serve my community.

What is or has been your favorite way to save money and why?
My favorite way is putting my money into a high-interest savings account when I have cash and investing the rest in a Roth 401(k).

What is or has been your favorite way to increase your income and why?
My notary signing agent side hustle has been my favorite.

What is your current savings rate?

My current rate is 25 percent.

Do you have a mentor and, if so, how helpful have they been in your FI journey?

I have a secret mentor, meaning he doesn't know he's my mentor, but he assists me a lot and is someone to look up to!

If you invest in the stock market, what is your preferred type of investment or method?

Mutual funds.

How many real estate properties do you own? What types are they?

I have one home as of now that I am house hacking. I had my home built in a new-build area where I speculated that property values would likely go up. I have rented out all bedrooms and the basement since February 2019.

Would you change anything about your path to FI? If so, what?

I would have purchased a duplex or triplex so that I wouldn't have to have roommates in my current house hack. However, duplexes and triplexes are much more expensive where I live, so I am happy with what I have now. My next investment property purchase will likely be a duplex.

What one piece of advice would you give a teenager who wants to achieve early FI?

I would first suggest that if you don't know what you want to do after you finish high school, go to a trade school! It will save you from getting into a bunch of debt and give you more time to think about what it is that you truly want to do in life.

PART THREE

THE KEYS TO FI

If you can't manage $1,000, you can't manage $10,000. You don't suddenly learn how to manage money by amassing more of it. This is why a lot of lottery winners lose it all. Financial literacy is not a side effect of wealth. Wealth is a side effect of financial literacy.

—INTERNET WISDOM

In Part Three, we'll start to examine some basic personal finance concepts. You can't achieve early financial independence unless you're financially literate. Chapters Eight through Fourteen explain some of the most critical topics for your early FI journey.

Since this is not a book about personal finance (there are many great books about the subject), we will explore only the most essential concepts. The FI Freak Checklist includes additional reading so you can learn all the concepts you'll need to become a true FI Freak.

CHAPTER 8:
THE COMPOUNDING EFFECT

Compound interest is the eighth wonder of the world. He who understands it, earns it; he who doesn't, pays it.

—ATTRIBUTED TO ALBERT EINSTEIN

Granted, it's a bit of a stretch to compare the splendor of the Grand Canyon, one of the seven natural wonders of the world, to a financial concept. But the powerful effects of water rushing through that beautiful canyon over time can indeed be compared to the power of the compounding effect over time. And time is one *huge* advantage you have as a teen.

We simply cannot talk about your financial future without talking about the compounding effect. It is one of the most important concepts we will cover. Compounding is most notably associated with interest, so let's first make sure we understand the concept of interest itself.

The Two Sides of Interest

You can *pay* interest or *earn* interest, depending on what you're doing.

For example, when you borrow money to buy a car by taking out a car loan, the bank charges you interest on the money you borrowed until you have paid that money back to the bank. In this case, you are *paying* interest.

On the other hand, let's say you have $1,000 in a savings account at a bank. The bank will pay you interest on that money as a "thank-you" for keeping your money with them. In this case, you are *earning* interest.

In both cases, one entity uses another entity's money, and they pay interest as a fee for being able to do so. The fee is called interest. It is usually expressed as a certain percentage per month or year.

FREAK
SPEAK

INTEREST: The cost of borrowing money, such as the fee you pay to receive a bank loan. Conversely, interest can also be money earned, such as the set percentage a bank pays you when you put funds into a savings account.

The Magic of Compound Interest

For my peers who are in the younger generation, you are sitting on a goldmine of time. Don't let it go to waste. Do something now to set the wheels of exponential growth in motion. That can be real estate or any other investment. Just realize that you have nothing to lose and so much to gain.

—JERED STURM, "STARTING NOW IS GOOD, BUT STARTING YOUNG IS GREAT: HOW TIME AFFECTS INVESTING," BIGGERPOCKETS BLOG

Most likely, you've heard about compound interest before, but you might not yet understand its real power. I'll try to put it into perspective: If the significance of smart money management were a tree, the significance of compound interest would be a forest.

 COMPOUND INTEREST: Interest paid on an initial amount *plus* any previously accumulated interest.

Let's elaborate on this concept by looking at an example.

Salvador has $1,000 that he knows he will not need for a long time. He decides to put it in an investment with an annual interest rate of 5 percent, which compounds every year. This means that Salvador will earn 5 percent of the balance in interest once a year, which is the benefit he gets for allowing someone else to use or hold on to his money. At the end of the first year, Salvador earns his 5 percent interest, which comes to $50. Now his balance is $1,050.

When the next year comes to an end, he will again earn 5 percent interest. But this time, instead of earning $50, he will earn $52.50 ($1,050 × .05). This may not seem like much of a difference, but compounded over several years, it amounts to a *huge* difference.

Here's a chart that shows what Salvador's account balance would look like after ten years. One line shows his growth (none) if he were to earn no interest—this would be the case if he kept the $1,000 at home, rolled up inside a sock or stuffed into an empty jar in the kitchen labeled "tea bags." Another line shows his growing balance if he earned 5 percent interest on just his *original* investment of $1,000 each year (known as simple interest). The third line shows his growth if he earned 5 percent compound interest.

Salvador's 10-year account growth

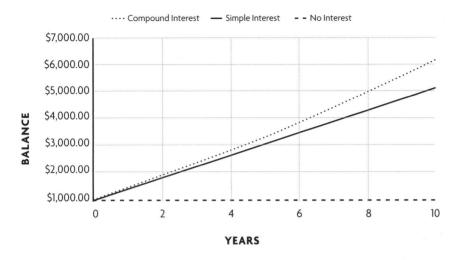

As you can see from the chart, after ten years, Salvador will earn about $130 more with an investment that pays compound interest versus one that pays simple interest.

Now let's see what happens to Salvador's investment over forty years.

Salvador's 40-year account growth

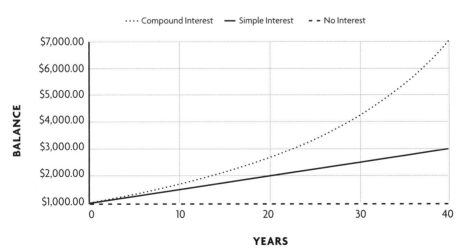

As you can see, the longer compound interest is at work, the more significant its impact. Instead of having $3,000 with simple interest, Salvador has more than *double* that at over $7,000! This is why you are in a prime situation to enjoy the fruits of compound interest—because you have lots of time! Most people don't see the value in compound interest until much later in life. Therefore, they don't start taking advantage of it until they are older, which doesn't allow compound interest to do its thing. Because you are still very young, you have decades to allow compounding interest to work in your favor.

The Compounding Effect in Other Areas

The compounding effect doesn't just work on interest. The intense power behind the compounding effect is the same force that creates exponential growth for several types of investments, such as stock market investments. Over time, those investments can see exponential growth as well, expediting your journey to early FI.

If you are wondering how to start taking advantage of this effect right now, good for you! Keep reading and we'll go over the two main ways a young person can use the compounding effect to their advantage. (We will talk about savings accounts in Chapter Twenty and index funds in Chapter Twenty-Three.) As you begin utilizing the compounding effect at a very young age, you will be maximizing its benefit for your future self.

CHAPTER 9:
REAL ASSETS VS. FALSE ASSETS

I put my money into things that increase my worth and passive income, instead of buying things that go down in value over time.

—STERLING WHITE, "THE NO. 1 REASON YOU'RE BROKE
(& HOW TO CHANGE YOUR FATE)," BIGGERPOCKETS BLOG
@STERLINGWHITEOFFICIAL ▶ STERLING WHITE

The Standard Definition of "Asset"

Once we understand the standard definition of the word "asset," we can start to look at how some assets are very different and why that's important.

The word "asset" can be defined as "something of monetary value owned by an individual." This definition is widely recognized and accepted. Using this definition, you could make a list of the many assets you own. This list might include:

- A car
- A collection of old baseball cards (or some other collection)
- Clothing
- Books
- A video game system
- A bike
- Furniture
- A guitar
- Cash
- Money in a bank account

We could go on, but you get the picture.

A physical asset has value if you can sell it to someone else for cash. For example, if someone is willing to pay you $3,000 for your car (or even $300, for that matter), it's an asset.

However, if you have no artistic ability and sketch an ugly picture of your neighbor's dog, that picture would not be considered an asset using the above definition because it has no monetary value. In other words, if you list that ugly sketch for sale on eBay, Craigslist, and Facebook Marketplace, no one will offer to pay you for it.

This is where most people's definition of "asset" ends. But a FI Freak knows that not all assets are created equal.

The Difference Between Real and False Assets

REAL ASSET: An asset that generates income or increases net worth.

FALSE ASSET: An asset that decreases net worth because of expenses or depreciation.

DEPRECIATION: A reduction in the value of an asset over time.

Understanding the difference between real and false assets is crazy important. The simplest way to think about it is that a real asset puts money *in* your pocket, and a false asset takes money *out* of your pocket.

Let's assume you own a gaming system. If you sold it to a friend, you might get $200. Does that mean it's worth $200? Yes. But as long as it sits in your room, its dollar value doesn't matter because it's not building wealth for you. As a matter of fact, every day it's in your possession, it actually *costs* you money because as it ages, it loses value. If you were to sell that same gaming system to a friend a year from now, you might get only $100 because it's a year older and doesn't have the newest features (or worse—the kiss of death—a newer model altogether has come out). This decrease in value is called depreciation. As time goes by, the gaming system depreciates, decreasing your net worth.

How about a car? Again, most would say a car is an asset—but based on our Freakish definition, it is not a *real* asset. A car doesn't make you money. Instead, it costs you lots of money just to have it. If you add up gas, insurance, maintenance, and depreciation, it can cost you hundreds or thousands of dollars a month.

But you might say, "I need a car! I'm not getting rid of mine!" Owning a car is not the end of your FI world. (I own one too.) You just need to realize it's not a real asset because it's not *making* money for you—it's *taking* money from you.

So, what's an example of a real asset? The answer is anything you own that creates income or increases your net worth.

For example, let's say you own a condo that you rent out to tenants.

The condo costs you money in the form of mortgage payments, property insurance, property taxes, and so on. However, what your tenants pay you to live there should cover those expenses and then some. Therefore, the condo is a real asset because it makes money for you. Real assets will provide you with income or build your net worth over time.

Here are some examples of real assets:
- A house that you rent out
- Stocks
- Bonds
- Index funds

And here are some common examples of false assets:
- A car
- Toys and games
- Clothing
- Computers and electronics

Many people are surprised to learn that if they own the house they live in, it is not a real asset. That's because a primary residence doesn't provide income. Also, tax write-offs and appreciation are often not enough to compensate for the expenses incurred by owning a property; thus, for the sake of FI, home ownership does not significantly increase net worth.

In fact, a typical primary residence takes money out of your pocket. You have expenses such as mortgage payments, insurance, property taxes, maintenance, utilities, and more. Those expenses add up to some big numbers. In fact, they make up the largest monthly expense for most people: housing. Owning the property you live in can help you along your journey to early FI—you just need to do it the right way. We'll get into real estate investing in more depth in Chapters Twenty-Four and Twenty-Five. A strategy called "house hacking" is the best way to make your primary residence a real asset, and we will discuss this topic more in Chapter Eighteen.

Knowing the difference between real and false assets is *crucial* on your path to FI. Let's go back to that gaming system you own, which is worth $200. If you keep it, it will be worth $100 a year from now, thus decreasing your net worth. But if you sell it today and invest the $200 in something that will earn you a 5 percent return per year, you will be increasing your net worth with a real asset.

 RETURN: The money made or lost from an investment over time.

I am not saying you shouldn't own *any* false assets. You just need to understand how false assets decrease your net worth and take that into account when deciding whether to acquire them.

Let's say you're thinking of buying a car. You understand that it's a false asset because owning one costs you money over time. To decide whether to buy one anyway, ask yourself whether the value a car would provide you is worth the ongoing cost. If the answer is yes, then buy it. If not, then going carless is the Freakish thing to do.

Real assets are the ones that will fast-track you down your road to early FI. You should be focused on acquiring as many of them as you can over the next few years. False assets will only make your journey longer.

CHAPTER 10:
GOOD DEBT VS. BAD DEBT

An excessive debt level is the life equivalent of handcuffs.

—JOSHUA KENNON, "TEACH YOUR TEEN FINANCIAL
RESPONSIBILITY," THE BALANCE

Imagine you went out on the street and asked random people, "Do you think having debt is good or bad for your financial future?" Most would say having debt is a bad thing, and there is a lot of truth to that. But not *all* debt is bad—some is actually good.

One way to look at debt is to see it as an obligation. Another way is to see it as an opportunity.

What Is Debt?

 DEBT (OR LIABILITY): Money owed to a person or company, usually in the form of a loan.

One critical aspect of debt may be obvious but deserves to be high-lighted: *Debt has to be paid back.* When you enter a debt situation, you agree to pay back the money you owe. Most people only think about the immediate gratification of the debt's purpose (buying a new car, for instance) and not the inconvenience of paying the debt off in the future. If people would stop and think about the long-term consequences of a debt purchase and how it will affect their future aspirations, they would likely think twice about the purchase.

Car loans, college loans, and credit cards are a normal part of American life—but not for you if you want to be a FI Freak. You should *never* take out a car loan (more on transportation costs in Chapter Eighteen). Use student loans only if absolutely necessary (more on that subject in Chapter Twenty-Seven.) And always use credit cards responsibly by consistently paying off the balance every month.

Unfortunately, most Americans use debt irresponsibly. They do not have a plan to pay back their loans on time and are often charged high interest rates in the meantime. Advertising has trained us to see debt as the go-to option to purchase the things we "deserve." Just look at these stats from Debt.org:

- More than 189 million Americans have credit cards.
- The average credit card holder has at least four cards.
- On average, each household with a credit card carries $8,398 in credit card debt.
- Total U.S. consumer debt is at $13.86 *trillion.* That includes mortgages, auto loans, credit cards, and student loans.
- Student loans continue to escalate, having grown to a record $1.48 trillion in 2019.
- American credit card debt crossed the $1 trillion mark in 2019.

How much of this is good debt, and how much of it is bad? What is the difference, and why does it matter? And what can you do to make sure you *only* have good debt?

Bad Debt

 BAD DEBT: Debt used to acquire a false asset.

Simply put, bad debt is debt used to acquire a false asset. Using debt to buy an asset that will then cost you money going forward is a double whammy. For example, let's imagine you buy a car using a car loan:

- Whammy No. 1: You will pay back more than you borrowed because of the interest on the loan.
- Whammy No. 2: This asset (car) is going to cost you more money in the future by way of depreciation, maintenance, registration fees, fuel costs, and insurance payments.

If you absolutely have to buy a car, the Freakish way to do it is by saving up the money needed *first* and then buying it with cash, thus eliminating the need for a loan and all that unwanted loan interest.

Good Debt

By now, you've probably guessed what good debt is—it is debt used to buy a *real* asset. In this situation, you are paying interest to a lender in order to use their money to acquire a real asset. Your goal is for the real asset you acquire to have a positive return that outweighs the interest you must pay the lender.

 GOOD DEBT: Debt used to acquire a real asset.

For example, let's say you buy a condo as an investment property, but to buy that condo, you borrow money by using a mortgage from a bank. The bank will charge you monthly interest for the right to use their money. Your monthly loan payment to the bank includes $250 in interest.

You start renting out the condo. Your tenant pays you $1,000 a month.

All your expenses (mortgage payment, interest on the mortgage, utilities, upkeep, property taxes, and property insurance) total $800 per month. You would then be making $200 per month in positive cash flow ($1,000 − $800 = $200).

The income from this real asset more than covers all the expenses, *including* the interest you must pay on your mortgage, and you are receiving $200 of positive cash flow every month. But this is only happening *because* you took on debt in the form of a mortgage—and that, my fellow FI Freak, is the kind of debt I will take all day long!

Debt is also good when you use it to invest in yourself. Imagine you want to become an electrician, but the program to get the required electrical license costs more than what you have saved. You could get a student loan to help pay for the cost of the program. After getting a job as an electrician, you might make twice as much money as before. The loan and the interest would cost you money, but it is good debt if the additional money you earn as an electrician is more than the interest you paid on the loan.

Student loans are not always good debt, however. Going to an expensive college and taking on massive amounts of debt to pay for it (which many people do) is generally *not* the best way to further your education and can be considered bad debt. We will talk more about student loans in Chapter Twenty-Seven.

CHAPTER 11:
CREDIT SCORE

Building your credit score is an essential strategy for achieving early financial independence. By understanding how your credit score can affect your life, you can turn it into an ally in your FI journey.

This chapter will talk about what a credit score is, how it's calculated, and the different factors that affect your credit score. When you begin working through the FI Freak Checklist, I will guide you through doing the right things at the right times to build up a respectable score. For now, you just need to understand the basics and their *extreme* importance.

FREAK SPEAK

FICO SCORE: Sometimes people refer to a credit score as a FICO score. These are essentially the same thing.

What Is a Credit Score?

Your credit score is a numerical indicator of your trustworthiness and likeliness to pay your bills on time. It's a three-digit number that can range from 300 to 850. The goal is to have a *high* score. Any score above 720 is considered excellent, and that's where you want to be.

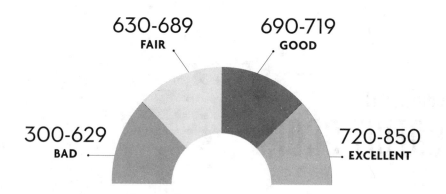

Three different bureaus compute credit scores for every person in the United States. Each bureau puts your financial history into an equation to arrive at a number. Your goal is to improve your financial history so that each bureau's equation spits out the highest possible number. Credit scores from the three bureaus are usually very similar, if not the same.

These are the three bureaus that compute your credit score:

Why Is a Credit Score Important?

Important is a *colossal* understatement. An excellent credit score is critical to your future. Companies and individuals will use your credit score to predict the likelihood you'll pay your bills on time, the likelihood you'll pay back money you borrow, the odds that you'll be a respectable tenant, and the chances you'll be a good employee.

Simply put, the higher your credit score, the less risky you are as a borrower, tenant, and employee.

Whenever someone wants to see your credit score, they must first get your permission. Then that company or person will ask each of the three bureaus for your score.

Companies and individuals will ask to see your credit score when you:
- Apply to rent an apartment or house
- Buy a car with a car loan (we'll talk about why this is a bad idea later)
- Apply for a job
- Seek a mortgage to buy real estate (either as a place to live or as an investment)
- Apply for a credit card
- Get insurance (e.g., car insurance)
- Inquire about starting a utility account (e.g., cable, cell phone, electricity, natural gas, water)

This bulleted list includes lots of activities that are crucial to your future life. Therefore, a good credit score will help you reach your goals much faster and with far fewer headaches. A bad credit score, on the other hand, can make all these things very difficult for you.

For example, a low credit score tells a lender that you are not very trustworthy and lending you money would be extra risky. They may very well deny you completely. If they do give you a loan, to compensate for that additional risk, they will charge you a higher interest rate that could cost you thousands of dollars in extra interest on a loan or mortgage!

How Do You Build a Credit Score?

All three bureaus that calculate your credit score do it in pretty much the same way. They arrive at a score by looking at the following five weighted components
- 35%: Payment history—Do you pay your bills on time?
- 30%: Amount owed—Do you owe a ton of money?
- 15%: Length of credit history—How many years have you been building your credit score?
- 10%: New credit—How many companies have asked to see your credit score in the last few months?
- 10%: Types of credit—How many types of debt do you have?

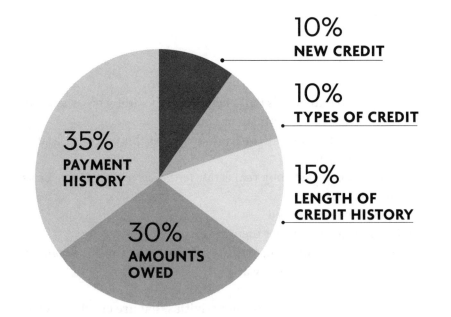

10%
NEW CREDIT

10%
TYPES OF CREDIT

15%
**LENGTH OF
CREDIT HISTORY**

35%
**PAYMENT
HISTORY**

30%
**AMOUNTS
OWED**

As you can see from this list, the best way to raise your credit score is to pay all your bills on time and keep the amount of money you owe low.

Even though many entities will look at your credit score before they do business with you, only a few of them actually report your loans and payments (or missed payments) to the credit score bureaus. These are the most common debts that get reported to the bureaus:

- Car loan amounts and payment history
- Credit card debt and payment history
- Mortgage amounts and payment history
- Student loan balances and payment history

Based on these options, you can see that the *best* way for someone young like yourself to build up their credit score is to get a credit card. But before you do, be aware that long-term *responsible* use of a credit card is necessary to build and maintain an excellent credit score. (We will talk more about this in the next chapter.)

You may have also realized that many typical bills do *not* help build a credit score. These include:

- Rent payments
- Utility bills

- Cell phone bills
- Internet bills
- Insurance premiums
- Medical bills

The companies and individuals that provide these services will check your credit score before you open an account with them, but once you have an account, they *won't* report your on-time payments to the three credit bureaus. These types of accounts don't help build your score because they don't involve debt (borrowing money). If you do *not* pay these bills on time, however, the companies can report your delinquent payment history to the bureaus, which will hurt your score. So even though they don't directly factor into your score, you still need to pay these bills on time.

Final Advice

Establish a habit of paying *every* bill on time, *every* time. Don't be late on a payment even once. Be Freakish about paying your bills on time so your financial goals will be easier to reach with a well-deserved high credit score!

CHAPTER 12:
CREDIT CARDS

You *need* to be using credit cards.

Surprised? That statement may not be in line with what many people are telling you. When the subject of credit cards comes up, you may be hearing words like "dangerous" or "harmful." But using this amazing financial tool is the Freakish thing to do. Credit cards are essential for your journey to early financial independence.

Before we get started, let's get clear on two important facts:

- Credit cards are *not* a source of income because they don't give you money. They are simply a way to borrow money that you *must* pay back later.
- If you don't use credit cards responsibly, they will actually prevent you from reaching early FI instead of helping you.

Credit Card Basics

Credit cards give you the ability to borrow money from a financial institution. That institution (the credit card company) will lend (not give) you money to purchase something.

Whenever you use a credit card, you agree to pay the money back. If it takes you longer than a month to pay back the money, you also agree to pay *interest* (extra money) on the money you borrowed. Interest is the fee you pay to the credit card company for the right to use their money.

Credit card accounts are known as *revolving debt.* This means the user can borrow money indefinitely, month after month, as long as they make the minimum monthly payments (which include interest), and they don't exceed their credit limit.

FREAK SPEAK

CREDIT CARD INTEREST: What a credit card company charges a card holder if they don't pay the total balance on a monthly credit card statement. The interest is added to the unpaid balance each month.

MINIMUM MONTHLY PAYMENT: The smallest amount a credit card holder must pay each month. This amount depends on how much money in total they owe to the credit card company. (For example, if you owe the credit card company $500, your minimum monthly payment might be $25. You can choose to pay only that $25, but whatever amount you don't pay off will incur interest charges.)

CREDIT LIMIT: The maximum amount of money a credit card holder can owe at one time on an individual card.

Credit cards allow you to buy something without paying for it right away. If you use a credit card to buy a new jacket for $200, the money doesn't come out of *your* bank account. Instead, the credit card company pays for the jacket. They will then send you a bill, and if you don't pay them the full $200 by the due date, they will charge interest on top of the original amount. Therefore, the longer it takes you to pay them back, the more money you will end up paying for that jacket.

Paying interest to a credit card company is the *last* thing you want to do during your early FI journey. It is possible to use a credit card responsibly so you never pay a dime of interest to the company. You simply must pay off the balance (the total amount you owe) each and every month before the due date. This allows you to access the benefits of credit cards, and there are many.

Six Reasons for Having and Using a Credit Card

- **Building your credit score:**
  This is the *most important* reason for getting a credit card. Making regular on-time payments to your credit card company will build your credit history and credit score. As we discussed in the previous chapter, a solid credit score is critical for getting a loan for a house, securing a job, or setting up a utility account.

- **Tracking expenses:**
  Every time you use your credit card, the transaction is recorded in your credit card account's electronic history. This makes it much easier to track your expenses, which is one of the most important things you can do to manage your money like a FI Freak.

- **Security against misuse:**
  If someone steals your credit card or steals your card information (identity theft), you are not responsible for the unauthorized charges as long as you report it promptly to your credit card company. The same can't be said if someone were to steal cash from your pocket!

- **Collecting rewards:**
  Some credit cards offer rewards for using them, like cash back or discounts on travel.

- **Covering emergencies:**
  A credit card can help you make a needed purchase in an emergency when cash or mobile payment options may not work. If you are away from home, get stranded late at night, and need to get a hotel room or have someone tow your car, a credit card will come in very handy.

- **Convenience:**
  There are situations in which having a credit card is simply more convenient than using debit or cash. For example, some establishments—especially since COVID-19—do not accept cash anymore. Further, many tourism sectors (e.g., hotels, rental car companies) often require a significant deposit if using a debit card. If traveling the world is high up on your happiness list, you'll find it easier with a credit card.

I will guide you through the process of applying for your first credit card at the appropriate time in the FI Freak Checklist. For now, you just need to understand that using a credit card will be a crucial part of reaching your goal of early FI.

What About All the Bad Things I Hear About Credit Cards?

You can have everything you've ever wanted in life—you truly can. It's all out there for you. But you cannot have it at 22. And someone will try and sell it to you at 22. And if you buy it at 22, you're going to be paying for it at 32 and 42 and 52. But if you wait, if you have a little bit of patience and you do the right things… you could achieve financial freedom very easily.

—ADAM CARROLL ON THE *NGPF PODCAST*
@ADAM.CARROLL

Credit cards *can* be dangerous if not used intelligently. To avoid the pitfalls of credit cards, you must follow two rules:
- Rule No. 1: *Always* pay your *entire* balance *every* month before the due date.
- Rule No. 2: *Never* charge more on your credit card each month than you can afford to pay off before the due date.

In other words, don't buy so much with your credit card that you can't follow Rule No. 1. Plan ahead to make sure you will have enough to pay the *entire* balance before the due date. But what if you don't?

In Chapter Eight, we went over interest, including the fact that you can both pay and earn interest. High interest rates are what makes credit cards so dangerous. Credit card companies can charge as much as 20 percent interest or more! When you don't pay off your entire balance each month, the credit card company gets to add more money to your balance.

People get into the most trouble by paying only the minimum required monthly payment. For example, say you buy a new laptop for $1,000 and charge it on your credit card. When the bill comes, you don't have the money to pay off the entire amount. You only have $300, so you pay that and leave the remaining $700 on the credit card. (They love it when you do that. "Bank" on it—pun intended!) Now the credit card company gets to charge you 20 percent interest on the remaining $700.

When you get your next credit card bill, your new balance is about $712 because of the added interest. The minimum required payment is only $15, which is what you decide to pay. (Why pay more than necessary, right?) Each month that goes by, you make the minimum payment and the credit card company happily adds some more interest to your balance.

With this awful plan (which is what many people use), it will take you about seven and a half *years* to pay off your debt. And you would pay the credit card company more than $660 in interest! This is *not* the way a FI Freak handles their money. You need a credit card, but you also need to use it correctly.

CHAPTER 13:
INCOME VS. WEALTH

Income can be taken away and can come and go. Wealth, on the other hand… is much harder to lose, and in many cases, increases forever.

—SCOTT TRENCH, *SET FOR LIFE*
@SCOTT_TRENCH

One of the most common challenges of personal finance is understanding the difference between these two critical terms: "income" and "wealth." As you begin to plan your journey toward early financial independence, we should take a moment to clarify them. Many people believe income and wealth are the same, but understanding the difference between them is vital for all FI Freaks.

Before we go any further, I should point out that "wealth" and "net worth" *are* the same. We mentioned net worth in Chapter Nine when we went over real assets and false assets. In that chapter, you learned that a real asset *adds* to your net worth, and a false asset *subtracts* from your net worth.

The Difference

The big difference between income and wealth is that income is how much money you bring in, and wealth… is how much of your income you've managed to hang on to and put to work for you. The less you spend, the faster your wealth accumulates.

—CHRIS SMITH, *I AM NET WORTHY*
@IAMNETWORTHY

Let's make sure you grasp the difference between income and wealth and why that difference is essential.

FREAK SPEAK

INCOME: Money received.

WEALTH (OR "NET WORTH"): The total of one's assets minus the total of one's liabilities/debts.

Your income is simply how much money you bring in during a given time period. For example, you might have an income of $100,000 per year. But there's an important truth most people don't realize: Even if a person has a high level of income, that does *not* guarantee they have a high level of wealth.

Instead, wealth refers to how much of your income you *keep*. If you totaled all your assets (things of value) and subtracted all your liabilities (money you owe), you would end up with your total wealth, or net worth. When calculating your wealth, you can decide whether you will include all your assets (both false and real) or only count your real assets. Most people who are pursuing early FI will do both. Therefore, they will have a net worth that includes their false assets as well as one that does not. They will then track both numbers, hoping to see their "real-asset-only net worth" grow over time.

Before we move on, let's quickly review the Four Mechanisms of Early FI:

1. Earn more.
2. Spend less.
3. Save the difference.
4. Invest your savings wisely.

Mechanism 1 is clearly all about your income. If you increase your income, you are earning more and are therefore optimizing Mechanism 1—but *each* of the Four Mechanisms will affect your level of wealth:

1. If you earn more, you increase your wealth.
2. If you spend less, you increase your wealth.
3. If you save more, you increase your wealth.
4. If you invest wisely, you increase your wealth.

The reason income is so commonly confused with wealth is perception. Most people in the United States who earn a high income also spend all or most of that income (that is, after all, the American way). This makes them look wealthy, but in reality they have a *low* level of wealth because they are not following through with Mechanisms 2–4. This is why some people who make lots of money (high income) can be broke (very low net worth).

Ed Sheeran (worth $278 million) and Taylor Swift (worth $400 million) are examples of famous people who have wealth. While they earn high incomes, they also manage their incomes wisely and use their income to increase their wealth. Not all famous people are as smart with their money, and they are proof that high incomes do not guarantee wealth. Both Aaron Carter (bankrupt in 2013) and Lady Gaga (bankrupt in 2010) were surprised to learn they were in massive debt because they overspent, resulting in a negative net worth.

Being wealthy isn't about how much money you make and spend; it's about how much money you make and *keep*. If you choose to spend most or all your income on expensive things so you can *look* wealthy, then you will have a challenging time building wealth. However, if you use each of the Four Mechanisms, including saving and investing a large portion of your income, you will build wealth fast. For most of us, it comes down to the following choice:

You can either *look* wealthy or you can *be* wealthy.

If you choose the latter, you still get to spend money and enjoy life! You just spend your money more intentionally and only on things you actually value. Planning to reach early FI does *not* mean you cannot spend money or have fun—you can do *both*.

How to Calculate Net Worth

[Net worth] can be expressed as a single number at any point in time, which means you can see… if your financial condition is getting stronger or weaker compared to previous measurements. And it means you can set goals—long and short term—and measure your progress toward them."

—CHRIS SMITH, *I AM NET WORTHY*
@IAMNETWORTHY

There is a simple equation for net worth:

$$Total\ Assets - Total\ Liabilities = Net\ Worth$$

To keep things simple, we will include both real and false assets in this calculation. However, you should remember that a FI Freak is more concerned with acquiring real assets than false assets.

The net worth equation provides us with a hypothetical situation: Imagine you sell everything you own and convert all your assets into cash. You then take that cash and pay off every person or business you owe money to, eliminating all your debts. The amount of cash you have left would equal your net worth.

Unfortunately, if most Americans did this, they would not have enough cash to pay off all their debts. That's because most Americans have a *negative* net worth. Too many Americans fall into this category because spending everything we earn and then spending even more with the help of credit cards and other consumer borrowing tools has become the American way. But a FI Freak will avoid this trap and build net worth instead of reducing it. The Four Mechanisms of Early FI are the keys to doing just that.

Most teenagers have a positive net worth because they've probably saved money from a job, an allowance, or gifts, and they don't have any debt (such as student loans, car loans, mortgages, or monthly bills). The few assets they do have put them in the positive net worth club. If this group includes you, congratulations!

The trick is to keep your net worth positive, never allow your net worth to become negative, and, instead, watch it grow steadily over time. This will be challenging for most of you over the next few years after graduating from high school. Big life choices like attending college, buying a car, and renting a place to live will significantly impact your net worth.

But turn that frown upside down! This book and many other resources will help you grow your net worth.

The most crucial benefit of knowing your net worth is the ability to track it and watch it grow. I suggest you calculate your net worth every six months and track it over time. Watching your net worth grow will motivate you to stay on track with your Freakish money choices.

CHAPTER 14:
PASSIVE INCOME

You will see that financial independence isn't just for the 1 percent or the 10 percent [of people making the most money]. It's for anyone and everyone who chooses to transform their relationship with money and accumulate enough wealth, which, when invested wisely, can provide a lifetime of passive income.

–VICKI ROBIN AND JOE DOMINGUEZ, *YOUR MONEY OR YOUR LIFE*
@VICKIROBIN

Understanding the power of passive income is paramount on your journey to early FI. In *Your Money or Your Life*, Vicki Robin talks about the idea that money equals "life energy." When we work our jobs, we trade our time—which is our most valuable resource—for money. In other words, you "pay" for money with your time. But what if you could acquire money *without* giving away your time (or very little of it)?

This *is* an option, and it's called passive income. Once you understand passive income and how it works, your life will never be the same.

FREAK
SPEAK

PASSIVE INCOME: Income you receive when not actively working.

ACTIVE INCOME: Income for which you must trade your time for money. Simply put, if you're not working, you're not making money.

Passive income is one of the most important concepts in anyone's early FI journey. (It is, after all, one of the three components of the FI Equation, which we briefly touched on in Chapter Three.) Pay extra attention to the ideas in this chapter, because passive income will be a crucial component of your financial future.

The Three Types of Income

Those who achieve early financial freedom build wealth and acquire assets such that they produce passive income in excess of what they need to live.

—SCOTT TRENCH, *SET FOR LIFE*
@SCOTT_TRENCH

There are three main types of income, and at some point in your life, you will earn money from each kind. You should be familiar with all three and realize that the second and third types are the best ways to build wealth and reach early FI. (In other words, No. 2 and No. 3 kick No. 1's butt.)

No. 1: Active Income

This is money you earn from working a job. If you babysit, wash dishes at a restaurant, or make sandwiches at the local sub shop, you earn this type of income. You will also earn active income, usually in the form of a paycheck, when you get a "real" job after high school.

The biggest downside to this type of income is that you don't get paid if you don't work. If you take an unpaid vacation, get laid off, or quit your job, the money stops coming in.

No. 2: Passive Income

Passive income comes in even when you're *not* working. For this reason (and more), it beats active income.

Now, passive income usually isn't 100 percent passive. It does require *some* work. But instead of working forty-plus hours for that paycheck, you may only have to spend a handful of hours per week managing your passive investments.

Unfortunately, most people never make *any* passive income. But not you—because you're a FI Freak! Earning passive income will be instrumental in your FI journey.

Passive income is the best-kept secret to building wealth, but building passive income streams is not easy. (If it were, everyone would do it.) It usually takes a bunch of work on the front end to enjoy the benefits for years after. The FI Freak Checklist will help you start earning passive income every month, so be patient for now. But know that this strategy will be extremely important to your financial future.

No. 3: Portfolio Income

Portfolio income comes from investments such as stocks and bonds. Portfolio income and passive income are very similar because they both help increase your net worth all day, every day.

Millions of people earn portfolio income by investing in the stock market in one way or another. Unfortunately, most people start way too late in life.

Does portfolio income sound overwhelming? If so, don't sweat it. By following the FI Freak Checklist, you will soon have investments in the stock market that will earn portfolio income. It's not hard to do; you'll be earning portfolio income very soon!

Different Types of Passive Income

I got into the business of collecting [rental] units... It's like having a bunch of those little candy machines that you put the quarter in. It's

*like the more you have, the more you make. So,
every [property] was like a little candy machine
[of passive income].*

—BRANDON TURNER, *THE BIGGERPOCKETS PODCAST*, EPISODE 345
@BEARDYBRANDON @BEARDYBRANDON

There are many types of passive income. Some may require a lot of upfront time. Some may require a lot of upfront money. Some produce more passive income than others ever will. For now, you can look at this list and start getting ideas of passive income streams that may work for you. (Oh, and by the way, this is *not* an all-inclusive list. These are just a few of the possibilities.)

- Buying rental properties
- Owning vending machines
- Owning self-serve car washes
- Owning laundromats
- Owning self-storage rentals
- Selling an e-book you've written
- Selling stock photos you've taken
- Selling an online course you've created
- Investing in dividend stocks
- Investing in real estate investment trusts (REITs)
- Putting money in high-yield savings accounts
- Renting out your garage
- Getting paid to put an ad on your car
- Renting out your car on Turo

Here's one more obvious example of passive income: the book you are now reading. Writing it involved a lot of time and research, but I enjoyed the process because I'm passionate about its contents. Now that the book is available for sale, I'm making passive income from it.

In other words, I'm earning money from this book without doing much of anything. If five copies of the book sell while I'm sleeping, mountain biking, or teaching high school classes, I earn money. (Please know that I didn't write this book *just* to earn money, but the passive income stream is undoubtedly a benefit I am happy to have.)

JABBAR ADESADA

@ @jabbar_investar
♪ @jabbar_investar

Where do you currently live?
Savannah, Georgia.

How old are you? Nineteen.

How old were you when you started actively pursuing financial independence? Eighteen.

What was your profession/career/ job when you first started pursuing FI? I was (and am) in the U.S. Marine Corps and a tactical air defense controller.

Do you consider yourself financially independent today? Not yet.

If you have not yet reached FI, at what age do you see yourself getting there? I would like to reach FI at 22–23.

Who or what got you started on your FI path? When I joined the Marine Corps, I had my first Thanksgiving away from home because I was still in training. A family graciously decided to host me for the holidays, and they were some of the happiest people I

had ever met in my life. I asked a few questions and learned they also happened to be financially independent. It didn't really take long for me to recognize the power of being financially free, and my mentor, Phil, started me on my journey with books like *The Automatic Millionaire* by David Bach and *I Will Teach You to Be Rich* by Ramit Sethi.

What is your Why of FI? I want to live my life with no regrets. The thought of a life bound by expenses and a thirty-year job scares me to death. I want the freedom to travel spontaneously and have as much fun as possible with friends and family. I don't want to be normal, and I don't want to live normally. I want to have an awesome life that I can control while focusing on helping others achieve the same. It is especially important to me that I make a long-lasting difference in the lives of those around me.

What are your plans for the future? I want to continue buying real estate investment properties so I can be financially free by the time my contract in the Marine Corps is over. I then want to focus on creating a seven-figure real estate business that will fund my acquisitions of larger multifamily deals. I want to eventually give away $1 million a year to schools back in Nigeria and impoverished neighborhoods in America so more children have a chance of living a greater life.

What is or has been your favorite way to save money and why? My favorite way to save money is the strategy of paying myself first. Instead of sticking to a strict budget, I just prefer to automate contributions to my savings account, tax-advantaged brokerage accounts, and individual investment accounts. It allows me more freedom to spend money on the things I value, because I know that my savings are automatically hitting my goals like a well-oiled machine.

What is or has been your favorite way to increase your income and why? My favorite way to increase income is buying it. I love cash-flowing assets, because you are essentially buying an income stream that theoretically should keep growing and last for decades.

What is your current savings rate? My current savings rate is 80 percent.

How many real estate properties do you own? What types are they? I own one real estate property that is a single-family home. I am currently house hacking this property, which means I am living in part of the house and renting out the other bedrooms of the house to young professionals in the area. After all my expenses, I cash flow just shy of $1,000 a month!

What has been your biggest challenge in pursing FI and why? My biggest challenge has definitely been my modest income. I have to side hustle and work extremely hard to be on track for my goals. But it has definitely enabled me to think outside the box, take risks, and grow my mindset.

What one piece of advice would you give a teenager who wants to achieve early FI? As a young person, you have the ultimate advantage: time! Your money has so much more time to compound the younger you start—so start *yesterday*! Take risks, because now is the time to make mistakes and learn from them. The worst thing that can happen is you fail and learn, which will help propel you to early financial independence. Also, the people you surround yourself with will determine your outcome in life, so start making friends with people who are doing the things you want to do.

PART FOUR

HOW TO PURSUE FI: EARNING AND SPENDING

We've smartened up. We've realized that the imaginary [corporate] ladder keeps you climbing inside the same trap that leads to being overworked and overstressed. We don't want to wait until we are too old to enjoy wonderful experiences like traveling or pursuing meaningful work... The curtain has been lifted, and we don't want to trade the best years of our lives so that we can have a few restful and relaxing years toward the end... We seek to build work around the lives we want, not build our lives around the work we have to do.

—ERION SHEHAJ, "FINANCIAL FREEDOM CAN MAKE YOU JUST AS MISERABLE AS YOUR 9-5 JOB—UNLESS . . . ," BIGGERPOCKETS BLOG
@INVESTINGARCHITECT

In Part Four, we'll take a deep dive into the Four Mechanisms of Early FI. We'll begin with Mechanism 1, *earn more*, and Mechanism 2, *spend less*.

Chapter Sixteen will go over several different ways to boost your income, some better than others.

In Chapter Seventeen, we'll examine the critical concept of frugality (or how to spend less money). We will look at why frugality is at odds with the traditional American Dream, and I'll go over some specific ways you can become more frugal today.

Chapter Eighteen will explore the biggest expenses you can look forward to after high school, and how you can minimize or even eliminate them. Finally, in Chapter Nineteen, I'll explain how to track your income and expenses and why doing so is critical to your early FI journey.

CHAPTER 15:
LAUNCHING INTO THE FOUR MECHANISMS

The path is so simple, and you don't have to go all out. You don't have to change your entire lifestyle. No matter when you're starting, just a few of these simple switches are going to give you a lot more options and choice and freedom in your life, and then you can do whatever you want with that. It's incredibly empowering.

—GRANT SABATIER ON *THE BIGGERPOCKETS MONEY PODCAST,* EPISODE 58
@MILLENNIALMONEYCOM

At this point, you are probably thinking, "I understand the concept of early financial independence, and I see how it can drastically change my future for the better. But *how* do I get there?"

The "how" is precisely what we are about to dive into.

Before we do, however, I want to share something really important: **You do not have to understand *everything* presented in this book to**

move toward early FI. As a matter of fact, I can pretty much guarantee you won't fully understand all the principles, ideas, strategies, and concepts we have already covered and are about to explore—but not because they are too complicated or you are not smart enough. The reason you won't fully grasp everything in this book is simply because it takes time.

The longer you spend focusing on your financial future, the more you will fully grasp the ideas and concepts that will lead you to early FI. I will try my very best to present them in a simple and easy-to-understand manner, but the fact is nobody—and I mean *nobody*—will get it all just by reading one book. So be patient with your understanding, but *do not* wait to get started. You can and should start on your path to FI now.

Think of it as driving down the road on a foggy night. The fog may prevent you from seeing more than fifty feet ahead, but you still can still proceed safely, so long as you are slow and steady. As you do move forward, the next section of road will become visible.

If you are motivated and dedicated to your future happiness, you will learn what you need to know as you need to know it, just as the driver on a foggy night can see what they need to see when they need to see it.

Remember when we went over the decision-making skills of an entrepreneur in Chapter Seven? You cannot wait until you have every piece of information to move forward, or you will wait forever. Don't let your doubts and fears keep you from becoming the FI Freak you are meant to be. For now, you just need a basic understanding of the Four Mechanisms, what they can do for your future, and what your next couple of steps should be. That's all.

Finally, as we get into the nitty-gritty, always remember to enjoy your journey toward early FI. The idea is not to struggle through a few years of hardship and pain only to find happiness *after* you reach FI. The journey itself should be fun and rewarding, thus bringing you happiness along the way. If you can't describe yourself as a happy person *while* you work toward early FI, something is wrong.

There is no way to happiness.
Happiness is the way.

—THICH NHAT HANH, *THE ART OF MINDFUL LIVING*

CHAPTER 16:
EARNING MORE INCOME

I reflected upon my habits and realized that I had wasted a lot of my own precious time. Hours were spent watching [sports], or mind-numbing TV, gossiping with friends, scrolling through social media—and quite frankly, this realization made me feel quite ashamed. Had I spent just 10 percent of that time on my own development and learning new skills, my career would have advanced sooner and my income would have been a lot more comfortable for me. Making the most of your time is one of the most important factors in success.

—ATCHUTA NEELAM, "9 THINGS I WISH I HAD KNOWN WHEN I WAS 20,"
BIGGERPOCKETS BLOG
@KOOLINVESTOR

Welcome to the chapter where the rubber meets the road: It's time to start executing a plan and moving forward on your path to early FI.

If you are going to get serious about achieving early FI, you will need to earn more (Mechanism 1). Some of you may earn some money, but only in the summer. Some of you may have no income at all. This will need to change.

First, though, you'll have to take a serious look at how you manage your time, because earning more money is going to take at least several hours a week. How much free time do you have? How much time do you spend watching Netflix and YouTube? How much time do you spend on Snapchat, TikTok, and Instagram? How much time do you spend sleeping in on the weekends? To become a FI Freak, you will need to manage your time better than the average teen.

Fortunately, there are lots of ways to earn more. This chapter will go over four income-earning categories, each of which includes several ideas you can start implementing now. As you read through them, look for one or two specific ideas that stand out to you based on your interests, skills, and schedule. Then try to implement them.

After making a serious effort to develop a couple of the ideas in this chapter, you may hit a dead end. Maybe there's no money to be made, the competition is too tough, or you decide you don't enjoy the endeavor. If that's the case, go back and choose another option. The point is to concentrate on just one or two at a time, because the more focused you are, the more likely you are to succeed.

Full-Time and Part-Time Jobs

A job is when you work for someone on a continuous basis and earn a steady paycheck. This category does not include odd jobs for which you may get paid irregularly, like raking the leaves in your neighbor's yard. It also doesn't include jobs (or random services) that are not performed for a business or company, like babysitting. (We'll discuss those later when we go over side hustles.)

Part-time jobs are typical for teenagers, but they could be part-time while you're in school and then evolve into full-time jobs on breaks and during the summer. Hundreds of jobs fall into this category. Here are a few of the most popular ones for teens:

- Official at little league sports games and sports tournaments
- Stocker or cashier at a grocery store
- Busser, dishwasher, delivery driver, server, or cook at a restaurant
- Office assistant
- Retail store clerk
- Ticket seller or taker at a movie theater
- Daycare assistant
- Personal assistant (type letters, run errands, file, do research, etc.)
- Lifeguard at a swimming pool

Working a part-time job is the most basic way to start earning some income. Even if you are extremely busy at school with sports, clubs, or activities, you can probably find fifteen hours a week to earn some money at a local business. Use your connections (friends, parents, parents' friends, teachers or other staff at your school, etc.) to get leads on possible part-time jobs. Also, keep an eye out for "help wanted" signs.

Next-Level Jobs

In Chapter Fourteen, we examined the power of passive income. In Chapters Twenty-Four and Twenty-Five, I will show you how real estate investing can provide quality passive income streams even when you are young. Why not start your real estate investing career now?

Here are some jobs that will introduce you to the world of real estate. Even if you're only fifteen or sixteen, I highly recommend exploring these options over the more common jobs we just discussed.

At a job related to real estate, you will be doing what Robert Kiyosaki calls "working to learn, not to earn." Though you will be earning a paycheck, the main benefit is the knowledge you'll acquire.

Assistant at a Real Estate Agent/Broker Office

Real estate agents can always use more help, and offices that house multiple agents need even more help. As a real estate broker assistant, you might be posting property listings, filing documents, greeting clients, answering the phone, and assisting with property closings.

Assistant at a Property Management Company

When the owner of a rental property doesn't want to handle the day-to-day responsibilities of managing their property, they hire a property management company to do those things for them. Just like with real estate offices, these companies can always use some extra help. As an assistant, you might help show properties to prospective tenants, work on marketing campaigns, fulfill maintenance requests, address tenant complaints, and check in on properties.

Assistant to a Contractor

Contractors are people who do maintenance and remodels on properties—everything from replacing flooring, to refurbishing a basement, to remodeling a bathroom or kitchen. Good contractors are always busy and usually can use some help. If you are handy (or would like to become handy), this could be an excellent fit for you.

Assistant to a Mentor

There is no better way to learn the ropes than to work for someone who does precisely what you would like to do someday. If you want to invest in real estate, maybe you or someone in your family knows a real estate investor you can connect with. (You can also find local investors by searching the BiggerPockets website.) If you want to work in banking or finance, maybe someone in your network knows a local banker or credit union employee who might need some extra help.

If one of these next-level jobs sounds interesting to you, start by searching for the appropriate type of business in your local area. Then go to that office in person, introduce yourself, and see if they might need a motivated employee. (Emailing or calling probably won't work.) Check out some YouTube videos on how to prepare, dress, and impress.

You could also seek out contacts through your network. Your parents can help by asking people they know who work in one of these careers if they might be looking to hire a hardworking teenager. Maybe one of your friends' parents works in one of these fields. Don't be shy about asking others to help you find a job you really want—they will usually be more than happy to assist you!

Jobs While in College

Some of you may already be in college, and others may be there very soon. There are a few jobs you can do while in college that will allow you to make the most of your time. Some of them even allow you to get paid to study!

Often, a job in the library can do just that. If things are slow while you're on the clock, you could be reading your class assignments while earning money.

The computer labs around campus need assistants to help other students and resolve certain issues. But these lab assistants are occasionally bored, with little to do, so once again, you could get paid to study. Talk about excellent time management!

I once heard of a student who worked at the front desk of their dorm. Someone had to be at the desk 24/7 to monitor the comings and goings. This student took the night shift, when there was very little activity, so they had plenty of time to study while earning money.

As soon as you arrive on campus freshman year, go to the libraries, computer labs, and dorms, and ask the employees how you can get a job there. Follow their advice to get one of these jobs where you can get paid to study in your downtime!

Another idea is to make and sell study guides for the tests in your large classes. Although this is not an actual job, but rather a side hustle, it still is a way to earn money in college while benefiting yourself; creating guides to sell to others is a great way to study for the tests yourself.

Side Hustles

 SIDE HUSTLE: A money-making activity one can engage in outside of being a full-time student or employee.

A job provides a steady income. A side hustle usually doesn't—at least, not in the beginning. But if you put enough time and effort into a side hustle, it can eventually provide an even better return on your time than a regular job. Instead of making $14 an hour working at a restaurant, you may find yourself making $1,000 a week with a legit side hustle.

Income-producing side hustles don't come easy. Since you will most likely be working for yourself, dedication and hard work are essential. If you put in the effort, a side hustle could become a massive income generator and optimize Mechanism 1. You'll never know until you give it a try!

Most good side hustles take time to get off the ground. The best ones require a bit of patience at the start before you see a return. Therefore, you may not realize a side hustle's income potential or scalability right away.

Your side hustle doesn't have to be something brand-new or completely innovative. Don't reinvent the wheel. You *can* make good money doing something other people are already doing.

Make sure your side hustle is something you like—or even better, *love*—doing. If you don't, it probably won't last. With no boss to answer to, you'll soon find yourself spending time doing something else if the side hustle provides no enjoyment whatsoever.

I will break our list of possible side hustles into two categories: easy-to-start and worth-the-work. Easy-to-start side hustles don't require much capital (money) or effort to begin. You can get up and running in a day or two. Worth-the-work side hustles have higher potential for growth or could generate more cash flow. These are usually not as easy to get started but can have a larger payoff in the long run.

Easy-to-Start Side Hustles:
- Babysitting
- Tutoring
- Driving for Uber Eats, DoorDash, Grubhub, etc. (18 and older)
- Shoveling snow in the winter and mowing lawns in the summer
- Teaching people of all ages how to use a computer, the internet, or specific programs
- Washing cars
- House-sitting while a neighbor is away (water plants, walk and feed pets, mow the lawn)
- Giving sports lessons (e.g., golf, basketball, baseball, soccer) to little kids
- Getting paid to put an advertisement on your car. Check out the StickerRide app or www.wrapify.com.
- Walking dogs or dog-sitting via apps like Rover and Wag!
- Joining focus groups (18 and older). Go to www.focusgroup.com.
- Donating plasma (18 and older)
- Getting paid to test websites. Try www.usertesting.com, www.userlytics.com, or www.userfeel.com.
- Sewing. You could make alterations, create costumes for children's parties, or produce custom-made pillowcases. Check out Etsy and Pinterest for ideas.

- Flipping couches. Many young people have found success buying used couches, cleaning them, and reselling them locally. This works even better if you have a vehicle that allows you to offer free delivery.
- Flipping other items. Some teens are having luck flipping items such as shoes, cars, clothing, and appliances.

Worth-the-Work Side Hustles:
- Developing websites or apps
- Fixing computers
- Purchasing a used vending machine, finding a new place to put it, and restocking it with purchased items when needed
- Buying low, selling high. Download the Amazon seller app and stop by the clearance aisle while you're out shopping. Check what those discounted items are selling for on Amazon with the app and see if there's money to be made. Craigslist can work too. Popular items to buy low and sell high are computer parts, bicycle parts, pet supplies, textbooks, smartphones, and athletic shoes. Or try something else you are very familiar with.
- Starting a yard game rental service. Buy a bouncy house or make some corn hole yard games and rent them out.
- Creating and selling an online training course or how-to video. Do you have a skill you can teach others? It could be crafting, dog training, or gardening. Consider creating an online training video and selling it to people who wish they were skilled as you. Go to www.learnworlds.com to get started.
- Teaching English. If you are a native English speaker, you have the skills needed to teach others your language. You will most likely be teaching people in other countries to speak English over the internet. Check out iTutorGroup, Englishunt, and Teach Away to get started.
- Selling a service on Fiverr. If none of the above ideas sparked your interest, there might be a service you can sell on Fiverr, where people will typically pay anywhere from $5 to $100 for tasks such as giving computer advice, creating a custom song on the ukulele, editing videos, and giving guitar or cooking lessons. Still don't have any idea what you would sell on Fiverr? Browse the categories for inspiration.
- Identifying a need and filling it.
  1. One young woman started urban hiking tours in her city.

First, she studied the history of the area and landmarks. She started by offering the types of tours she saw others providing—Segway tours, biking tours, bus tours. She found that she liked hiking tours best, so she expanded on that.

2. A young man found that parking lots in his town were dirty and full of garbage. He approached the lots' owners and said he would clean the lots once a week for a price. (Bonus: He can listen to podcasts and audio books while working.)

Nick Loper from Side Hustle Nation has even more ideas if you need some. But remember, you only need *one or two* ideas from this entire chapter to get you started on your FI Freak path to earning more income.

Side Hustles as an Investment

You may find that one of your side hustles or part-time jobs is a gateway to starting your own business. If that's the case and you enjoy the work involved, then a business can be one of the best ways to invest your money and accelerate your journey to early FI. As you think about one or two ways to earn extra income, consider choosing a money-making opportunity that could potentially evolve into a business of your own.

A new business doesn't have to be a new idea. Google wasn't the first search engine company, McDonald's wasn't the first burger joint, and Apple wasn't the first computer company. Think of how many pizzerias are in your town—only one of them was the first in your neighborhood. Most industries have more than enough room for multiple businesses doing the same thing. So if your passion is landscaping, don't be shy about starting a landscaping business just because others are already doing it. If the concepts about the entrepreneurial mindset in Chapter Seven resonated with you and you have the energy and enthusiasm to go down the entrepreneurial path, go for it!

Think big. Could the business grow more quickly if you hired an employee to do the work that's easy to pass to someone else? How much money would you need to invest in your business to help it grow until you see an acceptable return on your investment? What would the timeline look like for that? Are there others who can help you? Starting your own business can be an income-earning side hustle (Mechanism 1) that turns into an excellent long-term investment (Mechanism 4).

CHAPTER 17:
FRUGALITY

I drove a 1997 Dodge Grand Caravan with a driver's-side window that didn't work. It was taped shut for thirteen years. Whatever. I don't care. I own real estate. Get some.

—JOCKO WILLINK ON *THE BIGGERPOCKETS PODCAST*, EPISODE 365
@JOCKOWILLINK

On to Mechanism 2: Spend less. No surprise, this is all about decreasing the amount of money you spend—but before you get defensive and assume I'm talking about a life of deprivation and scarcity, please read on.

Although the word "frugal" has some negative connotations, living frugally is a positive thing. This chapter will examine how frugality can provide happiness and lead to early FI.

The Definition of Frugality

Waste lies not in the number of possessions, but in the failure to enjoy them.

—VICKI ROBIN AND JOE DOMINGUEZ, *YOUR MONEY OR YOUR LIFE*
@VICKIROBIN

FREAK SPEAK

FS FRUGALITY: Spending money only on things you value and not spending money on things you don't.

Is someone frugal if they own ten pairs of jeans? How about if they own three mountain bikes or an expensive computer with a 3D printer? Can someone be frugal if they take three vacations to Europe per year?

It depends. It all comes down to how much value each person gets out of those purchases. If those things rarely get touched or those experiences created little enjoyment, then chances are low that they made frugal choices.

But if someone has a job that requires them to wear jeans to work and they enjoy wearing all ten pair of jeans they bought, there's value there. If a person has a passion for racing mountain bikes and puts plenty of miles on all three bikes, there's value there. If a person started their own business printing 3D products and has success growing that business, there's value there. If a person writes a blog about places to visit in Europe, thrives on traveling to different countries, and makes money by selling ads on their website, there's value there.

In the end, only *you* know if a purchase will bring enough value and enjoyment to justify parting with the money needed to acquire it.

Frugality doesn't mean you can't have fun or enjoy life. While reading this chapter, if you ever think, "I could *never* give that up," then don't! Go ahead and spend money on the things you value—just don't spend money on the things you'll forget or regret.

Being frugal is not the same as being cheap. Being cheap means spending as little money as possible. Being frugal is about *prioritizing* your spending to have more of the things you value. Think of it this way:

Cheap = I don't spend any money.

Frugal = I spend money only on things I value.

Being frugal doesn't mean you can't buy that motorcycle or new coat or new shoes that you *really* want. If you value an item and fully understand its cost but still want to have it, buy it and enjoy it! But if you buy it and find that six months later you hardly ever touched it, you weren't honest about its actual value to you—or else you were blinded by consumerism and advertising that made you think you would enjoy it more and longer than you actually did.

Do you *really* value the latest iPhone? What if instead of buying the latest model, you bought a new iPhone on Amazon that is now the second- or third-oldest model? Would you be okay using that phone and saving $700? If you don't truly value having the newest iPhone, don't buy it.

What about subscriptions like Pandora, Spotify, Netflix, and Amazon Prime? There are so many media options that charge a monthly fee. If you have more than one, do you really use them all? Do they actually provide you with value and fulfillment? If so, great. If not, cancel them. That's being frugal.

If you cut your spending on things you *don't* value, you will increase your savings and thus increase your wealth (Mechanisms 3 and 4). This will put you on a fast track to financial independence.

Frugality vs. The American Way

We are spending money we don't have to buy things we don't need to impress people we don't even know.

—JOSHUA FIELDS MILLBURN AND RYAN NICODEMUS, AKA THE MINIMALISTS
@THEMINIMALISTS

There's one more thing you need to consider: your need to be accepted by your peers. Stop believing that people care what you have or what you do. Most people are too busy trying to manage their own lives to waste their time thinking about yours. Don't buy things to impress others. Only buy things that add value to your life.

We've already discussed the concept of enough. As a reminder, this is the idea that all we need to be happy is the security of knowing our basic needs are met, plus some comfort purchases and a few occasional luxury items. If we have those material things *and* the freedom of time, we can find more joy in our lives by doing what makes us most happy. (Refer to your happiness list from the beginning of Chapter Four.)

After a certain point, having more things will not increase our happiness—so while it's okay to have the latest iPhone if you value the enjoyment it adds to your life, you probably won't increase your happiness if you also acquire a new gaming system, the hottest handbag or shoes, and designer sunglasses. Having everything you could possibly want will not bring happiness or freedom. FI is not about having a lot of stuff; it is the experience of having enough *and* the freedom of your time.

However, we Americans have been trained (or maybe brainwashed?) to spend all the money we make. The problem is that this kind of lifestyle makes it virtually impossible to build wealth. The very first paragraph of the book *The Millionaire Next Door*, by Thomas J. Stanley and William D. Danko, illustrates why that path will not lead us to early FI. It says:

> *Twenty years ago, we began studying how people become wealthy. Initially, we did it just as you might imagine, by surveying people in so-called upscale neighborhoods across the country. In time, we discovered something odd. Many people who live in expensive homes and drive luxury cars do not actually have much wealth. Then we discovered something even odder: Many people who have a great deal of wealth do not even live in upscale neighborhoods.*

Why is it that so many people with fancy belongings lack real wealth? The answer isn't too hard to figure out. Those who spend loads of money on upscale houses, cars, restaurants, and vacations often spend everything they have and don't have any money left. While that may be an acceptable strategy for people who want to be handcuffed to the obligation of working for forty-plus years, FI Freaks are not on board with this plan.

FI Freaks decide to save and invest their money instead of spending it on luxury items. Those who choose to save and invest their money are able to build their wealth, and wealth is the key to reaching FI and no longer having to work. Meanwhile, many people in upscale neighborhoods will have to continue working until they are 65 (or older) to pay for all their purchases.

Frugality is also about enjoying what we have. As we consider acquiring new things and experiences, we need to ask ourselves if the pleasure and value they will bring to our lives are worth more than the money we must spend to acquire them.

For example, if you'd like to buy a new $500 Coach purse (or any other pricey item), first think about what it took you to acquire that $500. If you have a job that pays $15 an hour, you make around $10 an hour after taxes. So, it took you *fifty hours of work* to make that $500. Is that purse worth fifty hours of your time?

Second, you must ask yourself how *else* you could use that $500 if you didn't buy the purse. If you invest that $500, it might grow to $1,000. Are the enjoyment and value that purse can bring you worth more than fifty hours of your time *and* $1,000 in your pocket later?

If the answer is yes, buy the purse. If it's no, don't. If the answer is maybe, wait to make that purchase. After waiting a few days (or longer), if you still really want that purse, you should buy it. But if you've moved on, you probably just wanted it at that moment and are just as happy without that purse on your shoulder.

Specific Ways to Be Frugal

If you choose to spend 100 percent of your income on stuff, you are prioritizing that stuff over everything else. If you choose to save a large portion of that income and invest it, you're choosing to move toward freedom and flexibility as quickly as possible.

—CHAD CARSON, *RETIRE EARLY WITH REAL ESTATE*
@COACHCARSON1 @COACHCARSON1

Not all the ideas in this section will apply to you, but do read them all anyway to start training your brain to think about ways to save money.

Creative Ideas to Consider:

- If you value your gym membership, ask yourself, "What if I only pay for the membership during the months when it's difficult to exercise outside?"
- Instead of paying for a yoga class, you could offer to come early and help check people in or stay after and clean up in order to take the class for free.
- When you shop for something of value, consider thrift stores, Craigslist, Facebook Marketplace, or the Nextdoor app. Don't automatically pay full price for a brand-new item when a used item will do.

Things to Stop Doing:

- Buying things you don't need when they are on sale and telling yourself you saved money
- Allowing marketing messages to tell you what you value and what you should buy
- Letting what other people will think of you determine what you buy
- Paying for multiple entertainment subscriptions—instead choose one or two of those you value most
- Eating out often—cook at home with friends or family instead
- Going on shopping sprees (both online and in stores)
- Spending money at bars and clubs
- Always driving your car—carpool, bike, take the bus, use an electric scooter, or walk instead

Things to Start Doing:

- Put your cell phone on your parents' account and pay them your share (which should cost much less than paying for your own account).
- If you must buy new clothes, buy them at a discount store (Target, Walmart) instead of a high-priced retailer.
- Have a friend cut your hair.
- Give up brand names for items you need but don't value (toiletries, clothing, food, etc.).
- Instead of paying for activities, look for free options such as going for a hike, playing basketball, taking a walk with a friend, or reading in the park.

- If your parents want to buy you a new pair of brand-name shoes (like Nike), ask them if instead they could give you the money the shoes would cost (maybe $150) so you can buy a non–brand name pair (maybe $50) or a good secondhand pair (maybe $50 or less) and save the difference.
- Wait at least forty-eight hours before making large purchases. Take that time to ask yourself how you'd feel if you did not purchase the item. If you still feel you need it after forty-eight hours, go ahead.

Remember, frugality is not about living a life of sacrifice and deprivation. Buy and enjoy those things that add value to your life! But don't forget that when you choose to save money by not purchasing the things that *don't* provide value, you create more freedom for your future self.

Take pride in living a frugal lifestyle. Post a short video on all your social media describing a creative way you will be frugal. Then watch the other videos to get other great ideas! Or post a picture of yourself with this page and list your creative frugal choices in the caption.

Don't forget to use **#FRUGALFREAK** and **#TEENAGEFIFREAK** and tag **@ BIGGERPOCKETS** and **@SHEEKSFREAKS!**

I AM A Frugal FREAK!

CHAPTER 18:
THE BIG THREE EXPENSES

No one is rich whose expenditures exceed his means, and no one is poor whose incomings exceed his outgoings.

—ATTRIBUTED TO THOMAS CHANDLER HALIBURTON

Thankfully, saving money by being frugal is not as hard as you might think. It's all about how you approach it.

You may have heard that saving a dollar here and there is the best way to build wealth. For example, some people say that if you stopped buying that four-dollar coffee at Starbucks every morning, you'd save enough over time to make a substantial difference in your financial future.

I'm not on board with this belief, and here's why.

Let's say you do buy a four-dollar coffee on your way to school or work every weekday. Over a month, you would have spent approximately $88 ($4 x 22 weekdays on average per month).

Do those savings really matter? It depends.

The reason goes back to the idea of value we touched on earlier. If you truly value that morning coffee because it starts your day off with a smile, then buy the freakin' coffee! If it brings you joy, it's worth every penny. However, if you're just getting the coffee because your friends drink it and you want to fit in, skip it. If you could get as much happiness from making your own cup of coffee at home every day, consider doing that instead. Value, as always, is the key to the purchase decision.

Now, don't get me wrong. If someone gave me $88 each month, I would gladly take it. But I wouldn't be *too* excited since $88 alone is not going to dramatically change my life.

Let's compare that daily coffee to another expense: housing. Rents vary from location to location, of course, but fair rent for a young person might be $1,000 per month.

What if you could eliminate that expense without causing much, if any, decrease in your overall happiness? If someone wanted to give me $1,000, I would climb, stomp, and trample over any obstacle between me and that money!

The point is this: When it comes to saving money, it makes sense to focus on our largest expenditures and not the small ones.

The Big Three

Do not sacrifice your favorite small luxuries and recreational spending in pursuit of early financial freedom, unless your spending in these categories is obviously out of control. Instead, do big things right.

—SCOTT TRENCH, *SET FOR LIFE*
@SCOTT_TRENCH

Below is a breakdown of how much people spend on average for different categories of expenses. This information is taken from the 2019 U.S. Bureau of Labor Statistics Survey of Consumer Expenditures:

32.8%—Housing
17.0%—Transportation

13.0%—Food
11.4%—Personal Insurance and Pensions
8.2%—Health Care
4.9%—Entertainment

You will notice that housing is by far the largest expense for Americans. Next up are transportation and food. Focusing on lowering your expenses in these big categories will have a *much* more significant impact on your FI journey than limiting small purchases.

In this chapter, we will focus on these top three spending categories and how you can minimize them. We'll touch on a highly effective strategy called "house hacking," which can actually *eliminate* your housing expenses.

Does that sound too good to be true? Not at all. Remember, you're a FI Freak, and extraordinary things are what you do!

Housing Expenses

The amount of money we Americans pay for housing is our biggest expense by far. Most of us think we should rent or buy the biggest and most updated house, condo, or apartment we can afford. Well, if you want to work until you're 65 (or perhaps much longer), that *is* a great strategy. But if you're keen on early FI and getting decades of your life back, you will need to make better housing decisions—much better.

Since you are young, buying a property is likely a few years off. (Although not as far off as you may think—just wait until Chapter Twenty-Four.) After graduating from high school, you will have three housing options:

- Continue to live at home
- Live in a dorm or other school housing
- Rent a place to live

Living at home immediately after high school graduation is the best option, even if you pay your parents a small amount for rent. That small amount is usually a better deal than any other living situation you will be able to find. As a bonus, your parents may pay for some or all of the food, utilities, and other expenses while you're living there.

If you decide to go to college and the school is too far for commuting, you're probably looking at dorm life. You'll share a room with one or more roommates and a bathroom with even more people. Most of your utilities will be included—not a bad deal.

The last option, renting, is the least beneficial to your financial future; but if this is your only option, make the best of it. You'll have numerous options when it comes to renting, and many factors will affect how much you pay (location, roommates, amenities, quality, security, etc.). When choosing a place to rent, select an option that meets your needs with the lowest price tag.

Ask yourself these questions:

- Do you really *need* to live in the up-and-coming neighborhood?
- Is having a place all to yourself important to you?
- Do you really need that pool, workout room, or business center?
- Are the places you frequently travel to (work, school, grocery store) nearby so transportation costs can stay low?
- Are granite countertops and stainless-steel appliances (and other high-end finishes that drive up rent) necessary?

Here's a challenge for those of you who need to rent after high school: Sign a one-year lease on a place that pushes you out of your comfort zone, using the questions above to guide you. Find an apartment that's a little rough around the edges, is as close to work/school as possible, and allows you to live with some roommates. You'll pay a lot less rent than for one of the fancier options. Then, near the end of the year, ask yourself if the money you saved paying the lower rent was worth the perks you gave up. Most likely you will have become comfortable with your low-cost rental and thoroughly enjoyed watching your savings grow every month. If not, one year is not that long, and you can upgrade when the lease ends.

If you think you can't go without living in an expensive, luxurious condo in the hipster part of town, let me tell you a story about Phillip Lindsay.

Phillip grew up in Denver, Colorado. After graduating from high school, he went to college at the University of Colorado Boulder. It was an hour's drive from his home to the university, so he lived in the dorms and eventually in off-campus housing while attending CU.

After graduating, he got his first full-time job back in Denver. Phillip also moved back in with his parents, living with them for the first couple of years while working his new job. Why? To save money. Even though he had his college degree and a job, he still decided that saving money while living with his parents was a sound strategy for his financial future. He wasn't ashamed of living with his parents while his coworkers and friends lived in really nice condos and apartments around Denver.

Here's the shocking part: Phillip's job was with the NFL's Denver Broncos. And he wasn't working in marketing, finance, or public relations. He was a *player*, having signed as an undrafted free agent a year before. As a matter of fact, he was their starting running back! He was a professional athlete, and he decided to live in his parents' basement to save money. He went to the Pro Bowl his rookie year while living in his parents' house. I would argue he also should have made the Pro Bowl in frugality!

Phillip earned more than $500,000 in his rookie year but still made sure he was saving as much money as possible. He didn't let his teammates' choices or others' expectations dictate how much he should spend on housing. *This* is the kind of Freakish behavior that will set anyone up for early FI.

House Hacking

House hacking is by far the best housing strategy for young people pursuing early FI. Whenever young people ask me for advice, I always tell them to start planning for their first house hack right now. This real estate strategy will allow you to own an investment property at a very young age because of its many benefits—the most significant of which is the low down payment required.

FREAK SPEAK

HOUSE HACKING: A strategy where you live in one of the units or rooms of your property and rent out the rest, using your tenants' rents to pay your mortgage and expenses.

There are many ways to house hack. If you're excited to learn more about this strategy, you can Google it or read the book *The House Hacking Strategy* by Craig Curelop.

Here's the strategy in a nutshell: You start with buying a property.

Let's say it's a five-bedroom house. You live in the property and take one of the bedrooms, which leaves four empty bedrooms. You can rent those bedrooms to friends, classmates, or coworkers. No matter who you rent to, you thoroughly screen them. You check their credit history to see if they pay their bills on time. You do a background check. You get references from former landlords. You only choose tenants who will be fantastic housemates.

You use the rent you collect from your tenants to pay your mortgage and expenses. You get to live there *for free*. You do have to manage the property (which isn't too tricky when you're living there), but the benefits far outweigh those additional responsibilities.

Compared to *paying* $1,000 a month to rent a living space, the house hacking strategy would *save* you $12,000 per year! And that doesn't even include the other financial benefits of owning a real estate investment property, which we'll go over in Chapter Twenty-Five. (When talking about thousands of dollars, saving $88 per month on coffee seems a little insignificant, doesn't it?)

You don't have to be sold on house hacking at this point. Just keep it in the back of your mind as a possible strategy to *eliminate* your housing expenses and start your journey as a real estate investor.

Transportation Expenses

The most ridiculous way to commute to work [or school] is with a newer, financed four-wheel-drive vehicle that gets less than twenty miles per gallon, and to do this over a distance of more than ten miles each way.

—SCOTT TRENCH, *SET FOR LIFE*
@SCOTT_TRENCH

When you're young, having a car can seem like your ticket to freedom. However, if you remember our discussion from Chapter Nine about real and false assets, you already know a car is a false asset that takes money *out* of your bank account every month and decreases your net worth over time.

What is the best way to approach cars and transportation if you're a FI Freak and value your money and financial future? There are many options available, but let's start with two crucial rules. A FI Freak will *never* do either of the following:

- Buy a new car
- Use financing (car loan) to buy a used car
- Lease a car

Just in case that didn't sink in, here is my advice: Never, never, never, never, never, never, never, *never* buy a brand-new car! Did I make that clear enough? *NEVER!* Also, don't ever take out a loan to buy a car. If you don't have enough money saved up to buy the one you want, save more money or buy a less expensive car.

Now that we know what the rules are, let's explore why those rules exist and what other options are left.

Why You Should Never Buy a New Car

Millions of Americans love to celebrate their newfound freedom after high school or college graduation (or their first steady paycheck from their first full-time "real" job) by buying a brand-new car. Our society has brainwashed us to believe that the make, model, and year of someone's car somehow defines their worth, value, or success level.

It's especially easy to fall into this trap when a salesperson or banker informs you that you can "afford" that $600 per month car payment that comes along with the new car. They don't tell you the car payment will extend your FI date by a decade or more. Yes, that's right! Buying a brand-new car and financing most of its cost (as most Americans do) will add another ten or more *years* to your countdown toward FI.

How is that possible?

Most people think there are only two or three costs of owning a car. They can easily list the standard costs, such as the money needed to acquire the car (down payment), money for gas, car loan payments, and the occasional oil change.

But that's just the tip of the iceberg. Here's the rest:

- Sales tax when purchasing the car

- Insurance
- Depreciation
- Maintenance and repairs
- Annual registration
- Car washes
- Parking

Depreciation is a hidden expense few people consider when buying a new car. It's easy to overlook since you never have to "pay" someone for your monthly depreciation, but it is a reduction in the car's value and, therefore, a reduction in your net worth.

For example, if you went out and bought a new BMW 2 Series as soon as you landed your first well-paid job after high school or college, the price would be around $36,000. And the second you drove that new car off the dealership's lot, it would lose about 20 percent of its value. It would lose another 5 percent or so over the remainder of that first year. So, after one year, the car would have lost $9,000 in value, which comes straight out of your net worth.

When you add in all the expenses of owning a car, especially a new one, it is *incredibly* pricey, which is why it will push your FI date out by several years.

So How About a Used Car?

Buying a used car is a much better option, although it's still not the best. (Spoiler alert, we'll talk about that next.) If you do buy a used car, remember, you must pay for it in full—no financing allowed. In other words, you should save up the entire amount needed to buy that car without borrowing any money from anyone.

If you decide you *need* a car and have saved up enough money to buy one, here's what to look for to get the best deal possible:

- Buy a car that is between five and eight years old. This is the sweet spot because the car has already done most of its depreciating but is still new enough to be reliable.
- Research the make and model online to make sure the car has a proven track record of dependability.
- Buy one with low miles—less than 8,000 miles per year is ideal.
- Aim for excellent gas mileage. Anything above 30 miles per gallon is good.

- Choose a car that holds its value, which means it won't depreciate much from the time you buy it to the time you sell it. The cars that hold the most value are the most popular ones—think Toyota Corollas, Honda Accords, and Nissan Sentras.
- Make sure the car has a *clean* title, which means it has never been deemed a total loss. In other words, you want a car that's never been totaled in an accident.
- Make sure the car has a *clear* title, meaning the person selling the car doesn't owe money on it.
- Try to find a car with a low number of previous owners. One previous owner is best. The more owners a car has had, the more abuse it has typically taken.
- Check Carfax to see if the car has been in any accidents.
- Get a popular model; it will be easier to sell when you're ready for an upgrade. Think Honda Accords and Civics, Toyota Camrys and Corollas, Ford Fusions and Focuses.
- Once you've chosen a car, have a mechanic do a PPI (pre-purchase inspection) *before* the purchase.

Most people buy a used car from a car dealer or an individual. Buying from a dealer is usually less risky. Dealers need satisfied customers to stay in business, so they typically sell quality used cars. Buying from an individual can save you money because individuals don't have to pay for running a business, but they may not be as trustworthy.

You could also use a car broker (also called an "auto broker" or "vehicle broker"). Find a trustworthy one in your area by using a third-party website, such as Angi. Then tell the broker precisely what you're looking for (see the list above), and they'll shop around to find you the perfect used car.

But even a used car has many costs. Here they are for your enjoyment:
- Purchase price
- Sales tax when purchasing the car
- Pre-purchase inspection
- Gas
- Insurance
- Depreciation
- Maintenance and repairs
- Annual registration

- Car washes
- Parking

If you do buy a used car, take good care of it. Put reminders in your calendar or phone to take it in for regular maintenance and get oil changes when needed (about every 5,000 miles).

The FI Freak Option—Having No Car at All

Before you pull the trigger and buy a used car, consider what life would be like without one. And if you already own a car, seriously consider selling it and putting that money to work in a real asset.

If you recall, one of the biggest factors in choosing a place to live is how close it is to your job or school. The reason this is so important is the commute. Commuting can eat up valuable time and money. If it takes just thirty minutes to commute to and from your job or classes each day, that adds up to five hours a week. That's a lot of time you *could* be spending on your side hustle instead. Then there's the cost of the commute: gas, wear and tear on your vehicle, and increased maintenance needs.

What about not having a car at all? If you strategically choose a place to live that is close enough to your job or school, you could quickly eliminate the need for a car, which you now know is a money-wasting false asset.

Before it's too late, let me just say: *Do not gloss over or dismiss this option because it's too different.* Living without a car for just one or two years can bump up your FI date by a significant amount of time.

Here are the costs you eliminate by not having a car. I've compared the "no car" costs to the average annual costs of buying and maintaining a $10,000 midrange used car. Let your potential annual savings soak in.

Purchase price $10,000
Pre-purchase inspection $400
Sales tax $600
Insurance... $2,500
Depreciation...$800
Maintenance and repairs $400
Annual registration.. $550
Gas.. $750
Car washes $50
Parking..$20–$250
TOTAL ....$0 instead of $16,300

Yes, you would still have some costs even if you didn't own a car. After all, bikes, scooters, public transportation, and Ubers aren't free. But the overall savings—easily over $5,000 per year *after* the initial purchase—would be life-changing and Freakish.

Here are some alternative transportation methods that can replace a car:

- Walking (great exercise)
- Biking (ditto)
- Electric biking (also kind of fun)
- Electric scooter (ditto)
- Carpooling (does a coworker or classmate live near you?)
- Public transportation (you can read while you ride)
- Uber/Lyft (a last resort on a rainy or snowy day)
- Rent a car (for longer trips, but you must be at least 21 years old)
- Ask for a lift from a friend or family member (and maybe offer them an incentive, like that you will chip in for gas and/or wash their car for them every so-many rides)

At least give it a try for a couple of months to see what life is like without a car. After all, you can buy a car at any time if you decide you need one.

Earlier, I challenged you to choose a less-than-ideal housing option for a year. Do the same here. Before buying a car, commit to using the alternative options I listed above for a few months to see how it works out for you. At times, it will be inconvenient. But it can *also* be inconvenient to make insurance payments, schedule oil changes and tire rotations, keep track of maintenance, and deal with a potential accident. So give it a go, then ask yourself if the money you saved was worth it.

If you already have a car, commit to not using it for one month. You'll be surprised at how well you can get by *and* by how much money you can save! If you then decide to go fully car-less (good for you!), you can sell your car and use the money for investing in your future.

That brings me to the most significant benefit of going carless: You can take all the money you'll save and invest it for your future. Not owning a car for a few years can decrease your spending (Mechanism 2) by tens of thousands of dollars. And that will come in really handy when you're ready to start hammering Mechanism 4 by investing that money.

Food Expenses

Food is an expense you, as a teenager, can easily minimize because you probably aren't into fancy restaurants. That said, saving money on food can be summarized in one brief statement: *Don't eat out so much.*

Eat at home. You can feed yourself delicious, self-prepared food for very little money. If you don't like to cook or are worried about the time it takes to do so, make a schedule with your roommates so each of you signs up to cook one dinner per week for the whole house. Those who don't cook that day will do the dishes and clean up.

Make it a regular errand to go to the grocery store (or order your groceries online to be delivered if you don't have a car). Buy the items you actually need when they're on sale. Write up a list of the things you want before you shop and stick to that list. If buying organic or non-GMO foods is important and of value to you, find markets that sell these items at a discount.

Pack a lunch to eat at work or school. Do the same if you're meeting a friend around lunchtime.

If you're eating out with friends, have a snack right before you leave so you don't order as much at the restaurant. Most restaurants will split the bill by item, so you only have to pay for what you eat, and fast-casual and fast-food restaurants always have you pay individually. Steer the group toward a restaurant that is inexpensive. Since most young people don't have lots of money, this should be an easy sell. It's not difficult to find a low-cost yet somewhat-healthy meal when heading out.

"Food" also includes drinks, and "drinks" include alcoholic drinks. If you see yourself as regularly heading to bars and partying all night while racking up an expensive bar tab, change your thought process *now*. It will do you no good to save $100 on food during the week only to waste it all at the bars on a Saturday night.

CHAPTER 19:
TRACKING INCOME AND EXPENSES

The payoff of [tracking your expenses] is awareness. Just knowing where your money is going will make it more likely that you will not waste it. When you see that you spent more than $1,500 eating out last month, you'll be less likely to eat out automatically. And that will help you save money.

—CHAD CARSON, *RETIRE EARLY WITH REAL ESTATE*
@COACHCARSON1 @COACHCARSON1

You now have the wisdom needed to start hammering Mechanism 1, *earn more*, and Mechanism 2, *spend less*. It's now time to keep track of all the money coming in and out of your life. Once you know exactly where your money is coming from and where it is going, you can begin to adjust where necessary. You won't have to guess. You'll know. Those adjustments and that knowledge will pave your path to early FI.

To be a FI Freak, begin now tracking every dollar you earn and spend. You have a choice of several free and easy-to-use apps and websites that will help you do just that.

The Difference Between Tracking Your Expenses and Keeping a Budget

Tracking Your Expenses

Tracking your expenses is about tagging every dollar that comes in and out of your life. It is not difficult and can be incredibly enlightening and even a little fun. The apps that do this for *free* will easily categorize your expenses and income so you can see how much you're spending on things like food, gas, entertainment, clothes, gifts, and more.

Tracking your expenses means you can no longer spend your money blindly, and that's a good thing. Most people underestimate how much they spend on any given category. When you track your expenses, you know exactly where your money is going.

Budgeting

A budget is a roadmap of where your money *should* go each week, month, or year. It's a plan for how much you will spend and on what. For instance, you might budget $150 for eating out every month. While this can be useful, most people struggle to keep true to a budget.

In *Your Money or Your Life*, author Vicki Robin offers an excellent example for understanding the difference between budgeting and tracking your spending. She says that dieting is like building a budget, whereas mindful eating is like tracking your expenses. When you go on a diet, you follow a specific program and count calories, fat, etc. The program's goal is to lose weight, and it forces that change from the outside in.

However, with mindful eating you think about what you are actually craving. You pay attention to what your body is telling you it needs. Without that self-awareness, you might eat when you're not actually hungry and barely even taste your food. Mindful eating, like tracking your expenses, is an inside-out approach. Rather than imposing strict limitations that may be difficult to consistently follow (as with budgeting/dieting), the inside-out approach is about consistent, adaptable monitoring that is unique to your situation and needs.

The bottom line is that budgets are useful, and you should eventually develop one for yourself. But first you need to know where your money is *currently* going. That's why you should start tracking your income and expenses. That process will give you an accurate picture of your money flow and point out areas where you need to cut back.

Using an App to Track Your Income and Expenses

The Mint app, which I recommend, is *free*. Other options include Personal Capital, Wally, PocketSmith, and YNAB (You Need a Budget).

Each of these platforms allows you to keep track of your expenses, categorize your spending, input your personal assets, calculate your net worth, and much more. When you set yourself up on one of these apps, you'll connect all your accounts—checking, savings, investments, credit cards, loans. The app will then let you track bank, credit card, investment, and loan balances and transactions through a single user interface, as well as create budgets and set financial goals.

On Mint, once you have tracked your spending for a month or two, you can view what the app calls your "trends." By clicking on this tab and choosing a time frame (like "last month") and a category (like "entertainment"), you can instantly see how much you spent. Remember, you aren't reviewing the trends because you want to stay under a budgeted amount—you haven't set your budget yet. At this point, you just need to see the total you spend on each category to find out where you can do better by spending less.

That's why I stress tracking your spending before you set a budget. If you budget $200 per month for entertainment, you might be tempted to spend until you hit the $200 mark. But if you don't set a budget and you see you spent $200 last month, you're more likely to say to yourself, "How did I spend that much? I can definitely spend less this month."

Observe the amount you spend in each category every month and slowly adjust your buying patterns. As a teen, you probably spend much less than most adults. Still, as you track where your money goes for things like games, movies, gas, eating out, clothing, and electronics, you may be surprised at how much you are actually spending. If the number is a lot higher than you would have guessed, then let the adjusting to a Freakishly frugal level begin.

Remember, every dollar you spend should bring you value in return. If that dollar didn't bring value, then it would have been better saved and invested.

Lifestyle Inflation

Now, I will tell thee an unusual truth about men and sons of men. It is this: That what each of us calls our "necessary expenses" will always grow to equal our incomes unless we protest to the contrary.

—GEORGE S. CLASON, *THE RICHEST MAN IN BABYLON*

FREAK SPEAK

LIFESTYLE INFLATION: The tendency to increase your spending as you make more money.

Tracking your income and expenses will also help you avoid one of the biggest money mistakes Americans love to make: lifestyle inflation. If you carefully track how much money you are bringing in each month and precisely how much you are spending, you can make sure that spending doesn't creep up as your income increases.

We Americans love to spend everything we make, and we also tend to make more money over time due to increased education, raises, or finding a better-paying job. As our incomes increase, we also "inflate" our lifestyle by spending more money.

I love the following lifestyle inflation anecdote from Chad Carson's *Retire Early with Real Estate*. It's about a young person named Louis, who is seeking advice from a mentor.

One day, the old man [his mentor] asked him, "Louis, do you want to know how to become rich?"

"Of course!" Louis enthusiastically said.

"If you want to be rich, Louis, you need to learn to live on less than you earn. If you earn $40,000, live on less than $40,000. Got it, Louis?"

"Got it!"

"Next, you need to earn $80,000. But you need to still live on $40,000. Got it, Louis?"

"Got it!"

"Finally, you need to earn $120,000. But you need to still live on $40,000. Got it, Louis?"

"Yes, got it!"

"Louis, if you keep doing that, you can't help but become rich. And it will happen faster than you think."

Notice the old man didn't say to simply spend less than $80,000 when making $80,000. The amount of money to spend *remained* less than $40,000. This is key in avoiding lifestyle inflation. As you make more money, don't buy that nicer car or rent that bigger condo. Don't start eating out more often and at nicer restaurants. Don't buy high-end designer clothes and take more expensive vacations. In short, don't spend more money just because you can. Continue spending money only on the things you actually value.

Start by creating your tracking account on Mint or the app of your choice, connecting your financial accounts, and exploring the app's features. This app is your new best friend for keeping an eye on your money and net worth. Become Freakish about inputting all your spending and checking the app daily to watch your savings and net worth grow over time.

I hope you're now excited and curious to start tracking your expenses. It will be one of the keys to building your wealth and speeding up your journey to early FI. Start today.

SARAH WILSON

@ @gobudgetgirl

♪ @budgetgirl

Where do you currently live?
College Station, Texas.

How old are you? Thirty-two.

How old were you when you started actively pursuing financial independence? Twenty-six.

What was your profession/career/job when you first started pursuing FI? Journalist.

Do you consider yourself financially independent today? No.

If you have not yet reached FI, at what age do you see yourself getting there? By age 40.

Who or what got you started on your FI path? After college, I lost my job at a newspaper and found myself unemployed with $33,000 in student loan debt. It was terrifying. I decided I never wanted to be scared about money ever again, and I started a plan to aggressively pay off my debt and build wealth so my livelihood wouldn't be up to anyone else ever again. I paid off my debt, saved a huge emergency fund, started investing, continued to increase my income, and bought a duplex, which I'm house hacking. I save and invest more than 40 percent of my income.

What is your Why of FI? I want to stop trading hours of my life for a flat fee. I want the options and opportunities that having money gives me, and I never want to be dependent on one source of income that could go away at any time.

What are your plans for the future? I'm in my first house hack now and saving for the next. I'll make $600–$800 per month off this property after expenses once I rent out both sides, and I plan to purchase a larger multifamily unit next to increase cash flow and my portfolio.

What is or has been your favorite way to save money and why? I traded my hobbies that cost me money (roller derby, shopping, eating out) for hobbies that would make me money (YouTube, reading, pet-sitting, reselling). I also found that meal planning, shopping sales, and avoiding food waste at all costs save hundreds of dollars each month.

What is or has been your favorite way to increase your income and why? My YouTube channel, Budget Girl, has been a fantastic source of income and encouragement over the years.

What is your current savings rate? Thirty percent of my day-job income and nearly all of my business income after expenses.

Do you have a mentor and, if so, how helpful have they been in your FI journey?
YouTube has been my mentor. I watch Investment Joy, Graham Stephan, Meet Kevin, and anyone else who is willing to share about how they got to where they are. The BiggerPockets online community and books have also given me more knowledge and experience to learn from than a dozen college degrees. I've been lucky to have some good mentors in my journalism career and still hope to find one in the FI community one day. They're invaluable and if you find [a mentor], hang on to them.

If you invest in the stock market, what is your preferred type of investment or method?
Index funds.

How many real estate properties do you own? What types are they? Currently, just one property with two units (a duplex) that I am house hacking.

What has been your biggest challenge in pursuing FI and why? Starting with a low income and without any sort of knowledge about making money has been my biggest challenge. I was given no financial education or family aid, so I started on my own post-college with a ton of student loan debt. Digging myself out of that hole and then increasing my margins so I could get ahead was a real struggle. I'm lucky I was young enough that I still have decades to build wealth.

Would you change anything about your path to FI? If so, what? If I could go back, I would start with taking out fewer loans for college and focus on budgeting, saving, and building income streams.

What one piece of advice would you give a teenager who wants to achieve early FI? Just because you have money in your pocket doesn't mean you need to spend it. Start building multiple income streams now so you never have to rely on another person for your livelihood. Passive income is the best thing in the world. Keep learning and be smart. "Get rich quick" doesn't exist.

PART FIVE

HOW TO PURSUE FI: SAVING AND INVESTING

Earning a lot of money is not the key to prosperity. How you handle it is.

@DAVERAMSEY   THE RAMSEY SHOW HIGHLIGHTS

In Part Five, we will dive into Mechanism 3, *save the difference,* and Mechanism 4, *invest your savings wisely.* Chapters Twenty and Twenty-One will explain what saving is, why it's important, why so many people struggle to do it, where you should save your money, and how much you should be saving.

Then, Chapters Twenty-Two through Twenty-Five will explain the two main ways to invest your savings, the pros and cons of each, and why these two methods are the preferred ways of investing among so many who have already reached early FI.

CHAPTER 20:
SAVING YOUR MONEY

It's not how much money you make. It's how much money you keep.

@THEREALKIYOSAKIYOUTUBE: THE RICH DAD CHANNEL

Over this chapter and the next, we will explore Mechanism 3 and the idea of saving money. Although saving money may seem pretty simple, apparently for most adults it's not. One crucial statistic proves this: Around 40 percent of Americans do not have even $400 saved to handle an unexpected expense.

What Is Saving?

You have such a massive advantage [when you're young] that you're never going to have for the rest of your life. I really believe that if people take one decade and just really save, [they] can set themselves up for the rest of their lives.

—GRAHAM STEPHAN ON THE *BIGGERPOCKETS PODCAST*, EPISODE 316
@GPSTEPHAN GRAHAM STEPHAN @GRAHAMSTEPHAN

FREAK SPEAK

SAVING: Not spending all your money right away but instead putting some of it aside for later.

If you regularly put some money aside, that money will eventually grow. It's not complicated. And it comes down to one important rule: Don't spend everything you make.

Still, saving is something our society generally does *not* do. Instead, the attitude of many Americans boils down to: "Let's spend everything we make—and then some!" This attitude is why so many are in debt and don't have enough money available to pay for an emergency expense like a medical bill or an unexpected car repair.

Why is something that is so easy to understand so challenging to do? There are three reasons:

- We are encouraged ("trained" may be a better word) to spend everything we make.
- Our society is obsessed with keeping up with others' spending and possessions.
- Most people don't know how to start saving.

Let's examine each of these reasons and see how a FI Freak can overcome them.

Spending All of Your Income Is Fun...
but Expensive

Consumption seems to be our favorite high, our nationally sanctioned addiction, the all-American form of substance abuse.

—VICKI ROBIN AND JOE DOMINGUEZ, *YOUR MONEY OR YOUR LIFE*
@VICKIROBIN

Marketing and promotional messages are everywhere, telling us all about the next product we *need* or the next item we *should* get. Social media has made these messages even more widespread.

We spend a few seconds watching the TikTok for Nike. We pause for a couple of seconds on the sponsored Instagram post for Wendy's. We see our favorite celebrity raving on Twitter about their new, beloved energy drink. We don't always recognize that this favorite celebrity is a paid endorser and likely has never bought a single can or bottle of that beverage.

Ads show attractive, successful young people wearing designer clothes, dining at high-end restaurants, and driving luxury cars. After hundreds of exposures, our mind tends to align those brands and that lifestyle with our needs.

Today's youth are more likely to recognize these marketing messages for what they are than older generations, but that doesn't mean you're bulletproof. The messages work, and they work on *you*. Corporations and businesses wouldn't spend billions of dollars fighting for your Venmo transactions and credit card purchases unless those messages worked *really* well.

But don't be ashamed or embarrassed by this. The reason they work so well is because spending money is fun. And spending lots of money is lots of fun. Therefore, it's not difficult to convince someone they *need* a sporty BMW even if they can barely make the monthly payments. The thrill of driving that flashy new Beamer to and from work makes it seem worthwhile. We are easily trained to spend money because we enjoy it and new things are fun to have.

Let's look at a favorite advertising trick. I call it the "false savings lie," and it works like this: You see an ad for a new snowboarding jacket. It looks great, and it's a popular brand. You think, "I wouldn't mind having that!" The ad says that for the next week you can buy it for $200 even though the regular price is $350. "You'll save $150 if you buy it now!" the ad proclaims.

Not true. When you buy something for a lower-than-normal price ($200 in this situation), you do not *save* money. In fact, you do the opposite. Despite what the ad says, you *spend* money—and you'll have $200 less than you did before. Every time you buy something, you are doing the opposite of saving, no matter the price.

It's not just people who don't make a lot of money that struggle with saving. People who make $25,000 a year spend $25,000 a year. People who make $100,000 a year spend $100,000 a year. People who make $1 million a year spend $1 million a year. Why? Because they fall victim to lifestyle inflation and the spend-everything-you-make mentality.

If we look at professional athletes, we can see many examples of high-income earners spending everything they make and then some. They boast about their extravagant (i.e., wasteful) spending on their Instagram and Snapchat accounts. Many of them go broke as soon as their income stops flowing in, usually around age 30. Why? Because they spent everything they made (and, in many cases, lots more) and chose to save and invest very little or none of their income.

A 2009 *Sports Illustrated* article titled "How (and Why) Athletes Go Broke" said that 60 percent of former NBA players were broke within five years of retirement and 78 percent of NFL players were bankrupt or under financial stress after only two years of retirement. Many of these professional athletes decide to buy a super-expensive house, luxury cars, and flashy jewelry because they believe they can, and should, spend everything they make. Then something happens—they get injured or traded, they stop performing at a high level, a better player comes along—and the money stops flowing. They have no way to pay for the things they've already bought.

Many celebrities fall into this trap. Here are just a few of the dozens of famous people who have gone broke at some point:
- Mike Tyson (boxer)
- Allen Iverson (NBA player)
- Evander Holyfield (boxer)

- Scottie Pippen (NBA player)
- Marion Jones (track and field athlete, WNBA player)
- Darren McCarty (NHL player)
- Warren Sapp (NFL player)
- Hélio Castroneves (race car driver)
- John Daly (golfer)
- Johnny Depp (actor)
- 50 Cent (rapper)
- Aaron Carter (rapper)
- Lindsay Lohan (actress)
- Amanda Bynes (actress)
- Nicolas Cage (actor)

To be fair, many athletes and celebrities do manage their money well, and some even understand the power of saving and investing. Ryan Harris is one example. He had a ten-year career in the NFL and won a Super Bowl with the Denver Broncos. At first, he had no idea how to manage his large income, but then he started educating himself. Here's a bit of what he said in a December 2020 interview on the *NGPF Podcast*:

I started to see, especially in the NFL, how many guys got things wrong. How many guys wanted more cars than you can drive… Saving for my future was difficult. I was $30,000 in debt after making a million dollars, and I said, "How does that happen?"… I also started realizing the wealthy people in the locker rooms didn't wear the flashiest clothes, didn't have jewelry on, and talked about different things like this word "dividends."

@RYANHARRIS_68 @NEXTGENPF

Ryan turned his financial mindset around and became a FI Freak—someone who understands saving money is a necessity to achieve early financial independence. FI Freaks are willing to ignore those potent marketing messages. They realize their delayed gratification will pay off when they achieve FI and free up decades of their time.

Simply put, FI Freaks do *not* spend everything they make.

 DELAYED GRATIFICATION: The decision to resist the impulse of grabbing an immediate reward in order to obtain a more valuable reward in the future.

Don't Give a S**t About the Joneses

If you stop trying to impress other people, you will save thousands, perhaps millions of dollars. If you must, impress people with how much money you have saved.

—VICKI ROBIN AND JOE DOMINGUEZ, *YOUR MONEY OR YOUR LIFE*
@VICKIROBIN

The second reason we have a hard time saving is because of the all-too-human tendency to compare ourselves with others, aka "keeping up with the Joneses." This phrase originated in the early 1900s with a comic strip of the same name. In the comic strip, the McGinis family is in a constant battle to keep up with the success of their neighbors, the Joneses. Today the saying refers to the tendency to compare ourselves to our neighbors as a benchmark for success or social standing.

Worrying that we are inferior to our neighbors, friends, and/or coworkers if we don't have as much or more material goods as they do is one of the worst thought patterns possible. We frequently base our self-worth on how we compare to other people, and we believe that's how others determine our worth as well.

You can see this all over social media. The primary reason people post pictures of their fancy meal, beach vacation, new car, crazy night out, or flashy new outfit is so they can *seem* like they are keeping up with their friends and peers. And once their post is out there, their friends and followers now must post something to match or surpass the new benchmark. It's a never-ending cycle of one-upping each other that drives many to bankruptcy, depression, low self-esteem, and even suicide.

My advice is to go against the norm: Stop trying to keep up with your friends and peers. It's a no-win situation. There will *always* be someone with more Instagram followers and more TikTok views than you. Stop comparing yourself to others. Be your own self and enjoy what you have, even if it doesn't seem as fancy or impressive as what someone else has.

The truth is that the people posting all those pictures are most likely *not* as happy or content as they seem, which is why they feel the need to prove how great their life is. If you are genuinely happy and content, you have no need to prove it to everyone else—especially people you don't even know.

Frugality and saving will point you in the right direction because you are consciously deciding to stop comparing yourself to others. In the end, expensive possessions and experiences won't make you happy, especially if they're just a way to prove your life is better than everyone else's.

Instead of posting pictures and updates on social media about your pricey new item or experience, post about something you did that *saved* you lots of money. That's what a FI Freak would do.

It's Easy to Start Saving

The single most important thing you can do [to] improve your chances of achieving financial independence is to start saving early. Do it and do it now.

—CHRIS SMITH, *I AM NET WORTHY*
@IAMNETWORTHY

The third and final reason that many people don't save is that they don't know how. They've never been taught.

As you implement Mechanism 1, you'll start to see money coming your way. When that happens, you're ready to begin saving.

Let's take a step-by-step look at how to start putting money away using the most basic savings tool: the savings account. We'll also explore how to make the most of this tool's potential.

The Savings Account

You might have a savings account already. If you do, great! If not, it's time to get one. If you are under 18, a parent will have to open the account with you, but your name can be on it as a joint owner.

This next idea may seem obvious, but I'll say it anyway: A savings account is where you should put your savings.

The money you put into a savings account is different from the money you put in a checking account. Why? The answer is its purpose. Every dollar you possess should have a purpose. Some of your dollars will be for paying monthly bills, some will be for entertainment, some will be for buying that fun splurge item, some will be for investing, and some will be for your emergency fund. If all your dollars were in one checking account, remembering which dollars are supposed to be used for which purpose would be really challenging.

Money in your *checking* account should be for regular expenses. This is the money you use to pay your bills and conduct your everyday life.

Money in your *savings* account is money you plan to invest (Mechanism 4) or are setting aside for another reason.

The savings account's job is to keep your money safe in the short term until you have enough to invest. Knowing that the money in your savings account is *not* to be spent makes it much less likely you will spend it.

Additional Benefits of a Savings Account:
- It is extremely easy to open.
- Most savings accounts don't require a large initial deposit—some require as little as $25.
- A savings account will pay you interest. As of March 2021, the average interest on savings accounts was 0.04%. (It's not much, but it *is* free money.)
- If you regularly use your savings account to save more money,

you will find yourself reaching your financial goals much more quickly.

- Having money in a savings account will give you a sense of security. Knowing you have money set aside for an emergency and future investments will make you will feel more comfortable and protected.
- By putting money into a savings account regularly, you will accumulate funds to make investments for your future. In this way, your savings account is a launching pad for your investments.
- You can access your account with your mobile device anytime, anywhere. You can also transfer funds between your savings account and your checking account with your bank's mobile app.

More Than One Savings Account

Since every dollar you possess should have a purpose *and* you'll be saving for emergencies, investment, and something fun, it makes sense to have more than one savings account. That way accumulating money for different purposes is much easier. Luckily, opening more than one savings account is incredibly simple. You can even have several at the same bank! Just talk to your bank representative and they will help you get set up.

SAVINGS ACCOUNT NO. 1: EMERGENCY FUND

An emergency fund is essential for dealing with unexpected expenses or emergencies. Everyone should have enough money in their emergency fund to cover six months of expenses. This means that if you're living on your own and lose all your income streams, you should be able to support yourself for at least six months on your emergency fund. The good news is that once you've set aside that much money in your emergency fund savings account, you won't have to add more (unless you withdraw some of it).

Leave this money alone unless there's... you got it... an emergency. This fund is a safety net to protect you in case you lose your job, your car needs major repairs, you have unexpected medical expenses—or a pandemic shuts the country down.

SAVINGS ACCOUNT NO. 2: FUTURE INVESTMENT FUND

Once you've saved enough money to pay for six months' worth of expenses in your emergency fund, it's time to focus on your future investment fund. This is where the money you'll use to hit Mechanism 4—invest your savings wisely—will go.

To make the most of this savings account, you can set up automatic transfers from your checking account into your future investment fund. This is an excellent idea if you have a regular paycheck that gets deposited directly into your checking account.

For example, let's say you're paid by direct deposit into your checking account twice a month, on the fifteenth and the last day of the month. It would be best to set up an automatic transfer so that a specific amount moves from your checking account into your future investment fund a couple of days after each payday. (We'll discuss exactly how much you should transfer in the next chapter.) This creates a great habit of always saving part of your income.

SAVINGS ACCOUNT NO. 3: "FUN" FUND (optional)
When we went over the idea of frugality, we talked about how it's okay to spend money on things we value. If those things are small, regular purchases, their cost works itself into our monthly budget. But what about bigger splurges? After all, rewarding ourselves with something expensive is fine *if* we actually value it.

Once you have enough money to cover six months of expenses in your emergency fund and are regularly depositing a consistent amount of money in your future investment fund, you can begin to put money into a "fun" fund.

Let's say you've always wanted to travel to Italy. This account will help you save for that expense while not taking money away from your future wealth.

If you have some extra money in your checking account after paying your monthly bills and contributing to your investment fund, you can move that money into your fun fund (it's easy to do with your bank's app) and start saving for that trip. By adding money to this account only after you've contributed to your savings and future investment funds, you won't confuse your vacation dollars with other dollars and potentially cheat yourself out of future wealth.

Saving money is simple but not always easy. It takes discipline and hard work. But once your balances start to grow, those larger numbers will be a powerful motivator for you to continue saving and even increase your goals as you envision how those dollars will help you live your best life.

CHAPTER 21:
SAVINGS RATE

If you can easily get by on significantly less income than you earn, you open yourself up to an entire world of possibilities and opportunities.

—SCOTT TRENCH, *SET FOR LIFE*
@SCOTT_TRENCH

As we've seen, saving a bit of money here and there is not an effective way to build wealth. You must have a plan and a purpose. Once you have an eye on the money coming in and out of your life (by tracking your income and expenses) and have set up a place to keep your savings (savings accounts), you're ready for the next step: setting and measuring a savings rate goal to accelerate your path to FI.

What Is a Savings Rate?
A savings rate is simply the percentage of your income you save (rather than spend).

Money Saved ÷ Money Earned = Savings Rate

For example, if Katalina earned $3,000 in January and she saved $1,200, her savings rate for January would be 40 percent. ($1,200 ÷ $3,000 = .4)

FREAK
SPEAK

FS **SAVINGS RATE:** The amount of money you save divided by the amount of money you earn, expressed as a percentage.

Having a savings rate goal is one of the keys to maximizing Mechanism 3. That said, hitting a specific savings rate goal is easier for someone who has a *steady* income. A steady income usually comes from a full-time job. Since you are probably too young to have a full-time job, your income may vary each month, and some months you may have none at all. But don't worry—you can begin tracking your savings rate today with whatever income you do have.

We've discussed frugality and decreasing your big three expenses to widen the gap between what you earn and what you spend. Your savings rate is a measurement of that gap.

You're more likely to maximize the difference between what you earn and what you spend when there's a specific number to shoot for each month and year. Having a specific savings rate goal can motivate you to maximize your income and minimize your spending. The savings rate goal sets the target. Then it's up to you to make the necessary choices to hit that target.

Paying Yourself First

Paying yourself first is **the most important concept in this entire book**. There is no path toward early financial independence without it.

The businessman and author George S. Clason introduced this concept nearly a hundred years ago in a series of pamphlets that later became the iconic book *The Richest Man in Babylon*.

PAYING YOURSELF FIRST: Routinely and automatically putting money into savings and investments before spending on anything else.

When most people earn income, they typically allocate the money in the following order:
1. Pay for necessities (rent, food, etc.)
2. Pay for wants (entertainment, travel, etc.)
3. Save whatever is left

Clason's idea was to adjust those priorities so they look like this:
1. Save a specific percentage *first*
2. Pay for necessities
3. Pay for wants with whatever is left

By saving first, you are, in effect, paying your future self first. In other words, the very first "bill" you must pay each and every month is to your future self.

This straightforward but incredibly profound concept might be the first Freakish money tip ever recorded—and it can mean the difference between having to work until you're 65+ or reaching FI well before your 30th birthday. To reach early FI, you must establish a habit of paying yourself first by saving a certain percentage (savings rate) of all your income—*now*.

How to Calculate a Savings Rate

Let's look at the best way to calculate your savings rate. There are three simple steps.

Step One: Calculate How Much You Earned

Your money earned equals all your after-tax income for a given time period. After-tax income is the money you have earned *after* your taxes are taken out. For example, if you put in twenty hours at your part-time job earning $15 an hour, your income would be $300. However, your paycheck may only come to $200 once your taxes are taken out.

Sometimes you may receive income without taxes taken out, like cash you earn for a side hustle. It's a little more difficult to determine the after-tax amount in these situations. A good rule of thumb for a teenager would be to set aside 15 percent of this money to pay taxes later, when you or your parents fill out your tax return at the beginning of the following year. Therefore, you shouldn't count that 15 percent in your after-tax income.

Your after-tax income will include:

- All paycheck amounts (after taxes are deducted)
- All cash received as payments (after taking out 15 percent)

If you track your income and expenses using one of the apps we discussed earlier, it should quickly and easily allow you to see your income numbers for a given time period.

It's important to note that you will also need to exclude from your income any money you put into an HSA (health savings account) or a pre-tax retirement account (such as a 401(k) or a pension fund). However, HSAs and pre-tax retirement accounts would only apply if you have a full-time job with a company that offers benefits. It may be a few years before this applies to you, but it's important to keep in mind as you continue calculating your savings rate throughout your FI journey.

Step Two: Calculate How Much You Spent

Next, you will need to total all the money you spent over the given time period (the same time period in which you earned the income you just calculated). If you've been tracking your spending with an app such as Mint and accurately categorizing all those expenditures, you'll easily be able to determine your total spending for any specific time period.

For example, in a Mint account, you can analyze your spending for a specific month. The app will automatically add up all the money you spent during that month *and* tell you in which categories you spent that money.

You may not have opened an investment account (more on that in the next chapter) yet, but if and when you do, make sure the total amount of money you spent does *not* include money you transferred into any investment accounts. You shouldn't include any of this money in your spending calculations because you did not spend this money; you saved and invested it.

Step Three: Calculate Your Savings Rate

Once you have determined the amount of money you spent over a given time period, you will subtract that from your "money earned" number to determine the amount of "money saved."

$$Money\ Earned - Money\ Spent = Money\ Saved$$

Then you can calculate your savings rate for that time period using the equation we mentioned earlier:

$$Money\ Saved \div Money\ Earned = Savings\ Rate$$

Calculate your savings rate every month and record it in a Google Doc or something similar. I recommend putting a reminder in your Google, Outlook, or phone calendar to calculate and record your savings rate on the seventh of each month. It's a good idea to wait until the seventh so that all transactions from the previous month have a chance to show up in your tracking platform. (It can take a few days for a credit card purchase to appear.) Wherever you record your monthly savings rate, also include your total income, total money spent, and total amount saved.

Create another reminder to calculate your savings rate for the entire year. (A good day to do this is on January fifteenth.) If you have kept an accurate record of your monthly numbers, you can easily calculate your yearly savings rate. Record this in the same place as your monthly savings rate data.

You can then begin to follow your savings rate over time and use that as a motivator to save more in the future.

What Should Your Savings Rate Be?

To reach early FI, you *must* become a FI Freak when it comes to Mechanism 3. According to Statista, the average savings rate for Americans in July of 2019 was 7.6 percent. A lot of knowledgeable financial advisors recommend a savings rate of 10 percent. But with your frugal lifestyle, lack of need for expensive things, motivation to earn more, and desire for early FI, you are going to *crush* this number. *Your* savings rate will be at least 50 percent and possibly as high as 80 or 90 percent!

If you begin tracking your savings rate and notice it's closer to the average 7.6 percent than the 50 percent or more you should be striving for, take a hard look at your expenses. Review your expense tracking to see what items you can cut or reduce. You may also want to consider new ways to increase your income by working more hours at your part-time job or spending more time developing a successful side hustle.

While the savings rate calculation mentioned in this chapter is the most straightforward, there are different ways to calculate "money saved" and "money earned." Therefore, it isn't very meaningful to compare your savings rate to someone else's, because they may use slightly different calculations.

However, because *you* will always use the same calculations, you *can* compare *your own* savings rate from one period (usually a month or a year) to another similar period. By comparing your monthly savings rates against each other, you can see if you are saving at a consistent rate over time.

To reach early FI, it's important to set a savings rate goal for yourself. What percentage of your income do you want to use to pay yourself first? Calculate your savings rate this month to see where you stand. Then use the concepts we've gone over for Mechanisms 1 and 2 to maximize your savings rate in the future.

In the next chapter, we will begin looking at Mechanism 4, *Invest your savings wisely*. Maximizing your savings will then allow you to invest like the FI Freak that you are!

Take pride in your savings rate goal. Post a short video on all your social media telling everyone about your Freakish savings rate goal. Then watch the other videos to see how you compare! Or post a picture of yourself with this page and put your savings rate goal in the caption.

Don't forget to use **#FREAKISHSAVINGSRATE** and **#TEENAGEFIFREAK** and tag **@BIGGERPOCKETS** and **@SHEEKSFREAKS!**

My Freakish SAVINGS RATE GOAL!

CHAPTER 22:
INVESTING

Do not save money for the sake of saving money. Save money to invest it.

—SCOTT TRENCH, *SET FOR LIFE*
@SCOTT_TRENCH

Could you reach financial independence by just safely keeping your money in a savings account? Yes, but it would take you decades to get there. Because you don't want to wait decades, it's now time to learn how to make your money work for you.

It's time to start investing.

The Importance of Mechanism 4

By this point, you should know the Four Mechanisms for Early FI very well. To recap:

1. Earn more.
2. Spend less.
3. Save the difference.
4. Invest your savings wisely.

Although each Mechanism is essential, investing your savings is where the magic happens . . . over a period of time.

Growing your wealth will not happen quickly. Even if you use all the strategies in this book, it will still take a few years to reach FI. But those few years would be many, many years if it weren't for Mechanism 4. When you start investing the money you've saved, things really begin to take off. (Saving money and *not* investing will do little for you, but if for some reason you did stop after Mechanism 3, you would still be light-years ahead of most people your age.)

FREAK
SPEAK

INVESTING: Purchasing an asset with the expectation that the asset will provide income in the future or increase in value over time.

An investment is something you spend money on because you believe it will earn you even more money (a positive return) in the future. Normally, with active income, *you* must work to make more money. Investing, on the other hand, generates passive and portfolio income, which means your *money* is working for you. In other words, your money is growing your net worth without you having to spend time working.

Investing some of the money you've saved is essential for building wealth, and there are many, many different types of investments. Remember, as a teenager you have a massive advantage over the average person when investing: You have an abundance of time to take advantage of compounding. Most experts agree that investments should utilize the compounding effect by investing for the long-term, but how, when, and where to invest is not so universally agreed upon.

As your future investment fund savings account grows over time, you will be taking money out of that account and putting it into investments to grow your wealth. Over an extended period, these investments will provide you with much better returns than just leaving that money in a savings account.

For example, let's say you put $1,000 into a typical savings account with an interest rate of 1 percent—actually a pretty good rate for this type of account. After ten years, your savings account balance will have grown to $1,105. Making a little over a hundred dollars is not bad considering you did nothing except leave your money in the account.

But let's say you also invest $1,000 over that same ten years and it earns an average annual return of 7 percent. Over the same ten-year time period, your investment will have grown to $1,967! That's the power of investing and letting your money work for you. While both situations are taking advantage of compounding, the investment provides a higher return than the savings account and, therefore, results in a much greater increase in net worth.

A Review of the FI Equation

Remember the FI Equation?

Passive Income + Sustainable Asset Withdrawal > Living Expenses

Passive income (which we covered in Chapter Fourteen) is money you earn when you're not actively working.

Sustainable asset withdrawal is the ability to regularly withdraw money from an asset, such as a savings account or a stock market investment account. If this concept is not crystal clear yet, hang tight—we'll explore this idea in depth and look at some examples in the next chapter.

Living expenses are all the costs and expenditures that result from everyday living. These include housing, transportation, food, clothing, entertainment, and more. To know if you have met the FI Equation, you will need to know your average monthly living expenses. Luckily, you learned how to track your expenses in Chapter Nineteen, so you can now accurately calculate your average living expenses.

Here is the reason for our little review session: What you *must* understand at this point is that when you take full advantage of Mechanisms 1, 2, and 3, you can maximize Mechanism 4's potential because you will have more money to invest. Then, when you maximize the potential of Mechanism 4, you can quickly build your passive income *and* grow your assets for sustainable asset withdrawals. The more passive income and sustainable asset withdrawals you have, the faster you'll reach FI!

Invest in What You Know

*Never invest in a business
you cannot understand.*

—WARREN BUFFETT

Warren Buffett is a pretty smart dude when it comes to investing (understatement of the year). As of December 2020, his net worth was an estimated $84.6 billion. It's safe to say he's smarter than you (and me) *and* has more experience. So let's take his advice to heart and make sure we let that last quote soak in.

What exactly does it mean to understand an investment before putting money into it? The answer is simple: If you cannot clearly and concisely explain an investment to someone who knows nothing about it, you don't adequately understand that investment yourself.

Let's say you're considering gold as an investment. Now imagine a friend comes up to you and asks you to explain the pros and cons of investing in gold. How would you respond? Can you explain how volatile gold is? Can you describe how gold usually does in comparison to the stock market? Can you explain the difference between gold stocks and physical gold? Can you tell your friend how much gold is selling for today? Can you clarify what a gold certificate is? Can you explain the difference between gold bullion and gold coins? Can you go over the tax benefits of selling physical gold? Can you justify why you might have to pay a premium for gold? Can you explain why gold doesn't always move inversely to the U.S. dollar? Can you describe how gold compares to other precious metals?

If you can't reply to all these questions intelligently and articulately, then, according to Buffett, you have no business investing in gold. However, if you can explain an investment *in detail*, you can also decide whether that investment is a good option for your money.

Warren Buffett's Twenty-Slot Rule

I could improve your ultimate financial welfare by giving you a ticket with only twenty slots in it so that you had twenty punches—representing all the investments that you got to make in a lifetime. And once you'd punched through the card, you couldn't make any more investments at all. Under those rules, you'd really think carefully about what you did, and you'd be forced to load up on what you'd really thought about. So, you'd do so much better.

—Charlie Munger, explaining Warren Buffett's Twenty-Slot Rule

Buffett understands that the key to financial success is not the *number* of investments you have, but the *quality* of those investments. If they are high-quality investments, you will not want to sell them for a long time. These thoughtful, long-term investments almost always outperform short-term investments (even smart ones).

Because you need to educate yourself on each investment strategy you choose and you don't want to waste your money, I recommend starting with no more than two general types of investments when you are young. (Starting your own business does not count.) Over time, you can expand into other opportunities, but for now, simple is good and two is plenty. (The two general types of investments I recommend are index funds and real estate, and we will dive into those next.)

There is another investing tripwire that lands many people on their faces. As you move along your pathway to early FI, you will likely have more money saved than you ever had before. This could make you more inclined to take chances with your money.

You might feel like you have so much extra money that it's okay to lose some. Don't let that feeling change your risk tolerance! You do *not* have money to waste or invest carelessly. Always remember the time, effort, and sacrifice it took to accumulate that money in your savings account. Treat that money with respect!

Finally, always keep in mind that although the goal of investing is to make more money in the future, it doesn't *always* turn out that way. It's never a good idea to put all your money in one company or idea, because if that single investment fails, you could lose all that money.

RISK TOLERANCE: Your ability to psychologically endure the potential of losing money on an investment.

How to Invest to Reach Early FI

In the next three chapters, we will explore the two main investing strategies for reaching early FI. Both strategies involve real assets, which we went over in Chapter Nine. Remember, real assets *build* your net worth; they don't *subtract* from it. The two main investing strategies we will dive into are:

Index fund investing

Real estate investing

Now, I know what you're thinking: "If I follow good old Mr. Buffett's advice, I should stay away from these strategies, since I don't understand them!" But you have plenty of time to learn about these (and other) investment strategies before you're ready to invest. You're probably at least two years away from investing your hard-earned and hard-saved money. Although these methods may seem complicated and confusing now, after reading the next three chapters and following the research and training outlined in the FI Freak Checklist, you will be ready when the time comes. Let's get started!

CHAPTER 23:
INDEX FUND INVESTING AND THE 4 PERCENT RULE

Over the years, I've often been asked for investment advice ... My regular recommendation has been a low-cost S&P 500 index fund.

—WARREN BUFFETT, 2016 BERKSHIRE HATHAWAY ANNUAL SHAREHOLDER LETTER

Before we go over the two main investing strategies for reaching early financial independence, I want to stress that I will only be offering a high-level overview of each one. The purpose of this book is to introduce you to the concepts of early FI.

You should also do your own research about investing strategies and options. Just beware that there's some bad information out there, and that investing for early FI looks much different than investing to retire at 65. Make sure you're getting your information from multiple credible sources that you can compare against one another.

Every investment strategy has disadvantages, and some have more than others. One of the strategies with the fewest downsides is called "index fund investing," which is one of many ways to invest in the stock market.

It's now time to investigate what virtually all FIRE community members (and Warren Buffet) consider the best investment option available when it comes to the stock market: index funds.

What Is an Index Fund?

Let's start with the most basic element of stock market investing—the stock. Pretty much anybody can buy stock (shares) in companies like Google, Apple, and Tesla. If you own one share of Google, you own a small part of the company and that is an investment. The price of that share can go up or down. If you bought that share for $100 and sold it for $90, you lost $10 and had a negative return (a loss). But if you sold that share for $110, you made $10 and had a positive return (a profit).

FREAK SPEAK

STOCK: A slice of ownership in a company. For all intents and purposes, "stock" and "shares" are the same.

Buying shares of a single company isn't too complicated. So let's continue.

You can also buy shares of *multiple* companies with *one* purchase. For instance, you could buy shares of a few dozen companies for one price by using a mutual fund company. That company would invest your money into the fund (grouping) of companies for you.

They won't do it for free, however. They will charge you fees because they pay their employees to strategically pick the best companies to include in that fund. (At least, that is what the employees are *trying* to do.) This means the employees actively manage the fund.

MUTUAL FUND: A collection of stocks or investments grouped together so investors can easily buy shares of several companies at once.

ACTIVELY MANAGED MUTUAL FUND: A mutual fund that is overseen by a fund manager who spends time picking the stocks they believe will perform the best.

The value of that fund of companies could go up or down over time, just like the value of an individual stock. That change determines whether you have a loss or a profit on your investment when you decide to sell your shares of that mutual fund. However, because you own a piece of many companies and not just one, there is a lot less risk of your investment going down significantly. There is also less chance of it going up significantly. This strategy is called diversification.

 DIVERSIFICATION: Spreading your investments over many different options to lessen the chance of significant losses—aka not putting all your eggs in one basket.

The fees you pay to the mutual fund company may seem small, but they add up *big time* over many years. It's the compounding effect, only this time it's working *against* you.

Enter the index fund. An index fund is a type of mutual fund that is not actively managed by the mutual fund company's employees. You still pay one price for a slice of many companies, but you are buying a share of *all* the companies in a specific index (category). That's why index funds usually include many more companies than the average mutual fund.

For example, there is an index called the S&P 500. It is a grouping of the 500 largest publicly traded companies in the United States. If you buy into an S&P 500 index fund, you own a piece of all 500 companies. (A mutual fund, on the other hand, may have only a few dozen of those 500 companies.) With an S&P 500 index fund, there is no guessing as to which of those companies are good or bad choices; you get a piece of each regardless.

Like company stocks and mutual funds, the index fund's value can go up or down over time. That change causes you to have a loss or a profit on your investment when you decide to sell your shares of the index fund.

 INDEX FUND: A type of mutual fund with a large grouping of stocks that match the components of a financial market index, such as the S&P 500 Index.

To buy shares of an S&P 500 index fund, you still have to pay a fee to a mutual fund company. But since there is no strategy to picking *all* the companies in a particular index, no employees have to be paid for their research and expertise on the *best* companies. Therefore, the fees are a lot lower. (Try something like 0.04 percent instead of 1.2 percent!)

Let's look at one quick example of how crippling actively managed mutual fund fees can be to your net worth when compared to those for index funds. Imagine you invested $100,000 in a low-cost S&P 500 index fund and left it there for twenty-five years. Let's say it earned a 6 percent return every year, and the annual fees are 0.04 percent. (This is in line with the average fees for a low-cost index fund.) After twenty-five years, your index fund investment would have a value of about $425,000. Not too shabby.

What if you invested the same amount in a mutual fund with annual fees of 1.2 percent? (This is in line with the average fees for an actively managed mutual fund.) Again, assume there was a 6 percent return every year. After the same twenty-five years, you would end up with about $323,000. That's right: That measly 1.2 percent yearly fee just wiped out $100,000 of *your* money—around 30 percent of your return!

Whether you invest in individual stocks, actively managed mutual funds, or index funds, there is one more way to build wealth by investing in the stock market: You can also earn dividends. A dividend is money a company pays to owners of its stock as a way of sharing some of its profits with its shareholders. Some companies pay regular dividends, perhaps every quarter (three months). If you own shares in an index fund, you will most likely be paid dividends.

DIVIDENDS: The portion of earnings a company distributes to its shareholders.

Why Index Funds Are the Best Option

Index funds outperform [actively managed mutual funds] in large part simply because actively managed funds require expensive active managers. Not only are they prone to making investing mistakes, their fees are a continual performance drag on the portfolio.

—JL COLLINS, *THE SIMPLE PATH TO WEALTH*

Many people agree that putting money in the stock market is a solid investment. (Just ask that Warren Buffett guy.) But what you need to know is that index funds are statistically the *best* choice for long-term stock market investing. They're not sexy or exciting—they're simply the smartest choice out there.

However, many young people *want* sexy and exciting! So they experiment with buying stocks of individual companies, because sometimes the returns can be really good. But, as it turns out, they can also be really bad. These young people will buy and sell stocks daily, guessing whether a stock will go up and down on a particular day in the hope of making a quick profit. This is called "day trading," and it is *extremely risky.*

 DAY TRADING: The buying and selling of stocks on the same day in an effort to make fast money from short-term price fluctuations.

Some of you will have no interest in "playing" the stock market. Warren and I have just told you index funds are the way to go, so that's what you'll invest in. Nonetheless, some of you will need to see for yourself, and that's fine. You may even get lucky once, twice, or possibly three times. But eventually, after enough losses, you will come around to the idea that putting your money in index funds is the best way to invest in stocks. It is the simplest, most boring, and most strategic way all wrapped in one.

Still not convinced? Consider this: Millions of people study the stock market every day. Many of them have college degrees in banking or investing and have been doing this for decades. With all that knowledge and expertise, wouldn't you think they're more likely than you to pick winning stocks? I sure would. Many of these people are the employees I mentioned earlier who get paid to pick companies for a mutual fund. They are pretty good at their job, and that's why you must pay them fees to do it.

But even most of *them* can't beat the long-term average returns of an index fund investment. So why would you think you could do it better?

Remember Warren Buffett's advice: "Never invest in a business you cannot understand." Picking winning stocks is a "business" you cannot understand without a huge amount of knowledge and experience. Period. So why bother trying?

Buffett summed it all up for us in a 2017 interview with Yahoo! Finance:

> *Basically, any attempts to pick the times to buy or sell,*
> *I think, are a mistake for 99 percent of the population.*

Maybe you still want to try out day trading or investing in individual stocks. (I get it. I tried too.) Go ahead, but at least take this advice: *Only* invest money you would be okay losing. And know that the faster you come around to the index fund strategy, the better for your FI journey. Those of us who don't want to waste time and money hope to see you in the index-fund-only investing club soon.

The 4 Percent Rule and Sustainable Asset Withdrawal

By now, you know you can build wealth from an early age and get to a point where you can live life completely on your own terms—a position called "financial independence." To achieve that milestone, you need to accumulate a certain amount of net worth, composed mostly of your investments in real assets.

This section will introduce you to a calculation that gives you the number you must reach to achieve that milestone—the actual dollar amount you must have to attain FI. It's called "the 4 Percent Rule."

The basic principles of the 4 Percent Rule are pretty simple. They are:
1. Save money.
2. Invest it wisely in the stock market (index funds, for example).
3. Continue to do so until you reach your FI Number.
4. Take out 4 percent of your investments each year to pay your living expenses.
5. Enjoy FI and the fact that you never have to work again.

FS **FI NUMBER:** The value of stock market investments needed to satisfy the 4 Percent Rule and achieve financial independence.

Years ago, three professors conducted some research referred to as the Trinity Study. They wanted to see what would happen if someone continued to strategically invest their savings in the stock market. They discovered that there is a point at which someone would have enough money invested that they could start using that money to pay for their living expenses. More importantly, at this specific point, the money would last until they died, even if they never added more to the investment. This concept—having enough investments to live off forever—has since become known as the 4 Percent Rule.

Think of it this way. If you won millions in the lottery, you wouldn't have to work ever again, correct? Your winning lottery ticket would catapult you to a situation where you could live off the money you won until you died.

Since most of us won't win the lottery, we must earn, save, and invest money instead—but the principle is still the same. If we can put enough money into an investment and that money grows over time while taking advantage of compounding, there will come the point at which there is enough money for us to live an enjoyable, fulfilled life and pay all our expenses until we die.

In other words, if someone has enough money invested, they never have to put more money *into* their investment, even though they are taking money *from* that investment to pay for all their living expenses. Since that person would never have to put more money in, they would not have to *earn* more money to invest. And since they don't have to earn more money to invest, they would never have to *work* again. As you already know, that situation is called *financial independence*.

Once someone reaches their FI Number, they could withdraw 4 percent of their initial account balance each year and, with the help of the average return of the stock market, as well as compounding investments and interest, they would never run out of money during their life.

Let's do one quick calculation using the 4 Percent Rule. Suppose Abby has been working hard at hammering the Four Mechanisms over the past several years. She now has $2 million invested in her index fund. If she used the 4 Percent Rule, her calculation would look like this:

$$\$2,000,000 \times .04 = \$80,000$$

This tells Abby that if she stopped putting money into the index fund investment and started living off that investment by taking out 4 percent ($80,000) each year until she died, she would not run out of money. Abby needs to ask herself if she could live off $80,000 per year; if so, she's reached her FI Number.

Most people want to know their FI Number first, however. They just need to change the equation a bit. Suppose Sannibel has been tracking her income and expenses for a couple of years. When looking at her spending numbers, she is confident that $40,000 will pay for her annual living expenses. Knowing this, she could calculate her FI Number using this equation:

Annual Expenses ÷ .04 = FI Number

Therefore, Sanibel's calculation looks like this:

$40,000 ÷ .04 = $1 million

This tells Sannibel that she needs to have $1 million in her index fund to reach financial independence.

In the Trinity Study, the researchers assumed someone would retire around age 60 and live to around age 90, so they would need their money to last for thirty years. You will need your money to last longer since you will be reaching early FI *way* before age 60, but the basic principle is the same. There is still a magic amount of money (FI Number) you need to have invested that would allow you to stop working.

Unfortunately, it is too early for you to calculate your FI Number—you'll have to wait a few years. Once you are out in the world, you'll have a better idea of what your living expenses will be and how you would prefer to divide your money into passive income investments and index fund investments.

Be patient. As a teen, your focus should be on learning about early FI, saving, and investing.

Using the Whole Equation

Let's look at the FI Equation again:

Passive Income + Sustainable Asset Withdrawals > Living Expenses

Taking money out of some investments to pay for living expenses (the 4 Percent Rule) is precisely what we mean by "sustainable asset withdrawals." Once we reach our FI Number, we can sustainably take money from that asset (index fund) to pay for our living expenses without ever putting more money back in.

Now you may be asking, "What about the 'passive income' part of the equation?" Great question! Passive income (explained in Chapter Fourteen) includes all of the income we make that does not require our time (or little of it). The FI Equation tells us we can add our passive income *and* our sustainable asset withdrawal from money we've already saved and invested to cover our living expenses. You can and should combine them.

If you were building only passive income streams (such as rental property income and selling an online course you developed), you would reach FI as soon as you consistently had more passive income coming in than you had money going out for expenses. If, on the other hand, you relied only on the accumulated value of index funds and similar investments, you would reach FI when you had enough invested to pay your expenses using regular withdrawals from those investments. (Stay tuned for the next chapter, where we'll talk about how real estate investing can build passive income.)

FI Freaks use both. As you grow your passive income, the amount you need in sustainable asset withdrawals goes down—and the opposite is true too. The more you have invested in index funds and similar investments, the less regular passive income you will need to reach FI. Using both helps you diversify your investments, which is why a FI Freak should focus on both.

Also note that active income is not included because it's earned when you trade your time for money. If the main benefit of FI is *not* having to work, then we cannot include the income we receive only when we work!

How to Start Investing in an Index Fund

The sooner you start investing, the better. However, depending on your age and situation, you may not be ready to start investing in an index fund just yet, and that's okay. For now, just focus on the first three Mechanisms, and you'll be ready to invest in no time.

But if you *are* ready to start, here's what you need to know. If you are

18 or older, you can do it on your own. If you are under 18, you will need to have a parent open an account with you. (Oh, and you'll also need to have some money saved up.)

One more thing, and this is *crucial*: You should only invest in the stock market for the long term. In other words, you should plan on leaving whatever money you put into an index fund untouched for at least ten years. If you think you'll need that money for something else (like starting or boosting a business) in less than ten years, you should leave it in your future investment savings account instead.

 BROKERAGE FIRM: A business that acts as a middleman connecting buyers and sellers to facilitate a transaction.

BROKERAGE ACCOUNT: Similar to a bank account, but with a brokerage firm.

How to Invest in an Index Fund:

1. Open a brokerage account at Charles Schwab, Fidelity, or Vanguard using the firm's website. All three are trusted nationwide brokerage firms that have been around for a long time.
2. Transfer money into your new brokerage account from your future investment savings account.
3. Once the money has been received and verified in your new brokerage account, invest it in a low-cost index fund.

The following are examples of a low-cost index fund that was available at each of those firms at the time of this writing:

- Charles Schwab: Schwab S&P 500 Index Fund (SWPPX)
- Fidelity: Fidelity 500 Index Fund (FXAIX)
- Vanguard: Vanguard 500 Index Fund Admiral Shares (VFIAX)

Keep in mind that you may need help with these steps. If there's a parent or other adult who can help you set up the online account, ask them to assist you. If not, you can always call the brokerage firm you've selected and someone there can walk you through the process of setting up your account, transferring money into the account, and then investing that money in an index fund. It might be a bit intimidating, but don't avoid doing this if you are ready! Everyone's first time investing is scary, and you are doing it about a *decade* before most of your peers. So go easy on yourself and ask for help. That's what FI Freaks do.

Different brokerage firms have different minimum investments for their variety of offerings. A minimum investment is just as it sounds—it's the smallest amount you can invest. The minimum investment for these index funds I've listed here can range from $1 to $3,000 or more. Depending on how much you have saved and are ready to invest, you may be okay with a higher minimum investment. If you only want to invest a few hundred dollars, you can check online or call the brokerage firm to see what the current minimum investment is and whether that works for you.

Remember, the money you invest should be money you will *not* need for at least ten years. If you don't have money that falls into this category right now, wait. Even if you make your first index fund investment in two or three years, you will be *way* ahead of most people.

In general, the best strategy for these investments is to regularly put money in and let the stock market do its thing over many years. In other words, a smart investor will leave the money alone.

As we all know, the stock market goes up and down. If you frequently monitor your investment, you may panic when you see a drop in value and be tempted to remove your money. That would be a mistake, because over the long haul, it's a very safe bet your money will grow and grow.

In fact, the long-term average returns of index funds are your *best* bet in the stock market. You just need to be able to weather the ups and downs, and that's easiest to do if you aren't constantly watching.

Once you start investing money in an index fund, you are officially using Mechanism 4. Congratulations! You've begun to build your wealth and invest in your financial future. You are officially getting your Freak on!

Cryptocurrencies

We probably shouldn't move on before talking about cryptocurrencies. Many young people are forgoing traditional stock market investments for shares of Bitcoin or some other "hot" crypto. Remember Warren Buffett's advice about not investing in what you don't fully understand? Investors who get swept up in the cryptocurrency tornado often find themselves with empty pockets. If you are thinking of investing in cryptocurrencies (and I'm not saying you shouldn't), make sure you thoroughly understand them.

Test your knowledge. Go to one of your parents and ask them if they understand how cryptocurrencies work. If they don't, explain it to them. When you're done, ask them if they now understand cryptocurrencies. If they still don't, you probably don't fully understand them yourself, and you should either do more research or stay out of cryptocurrencies altogether.

Why Some Traditional Investing Options May Not Work for You

One thing we haven't touched on is retirement accounts. There are several types of retirement accounts through which people invest money to help pay for their living expenses after they retire. A retirement account is not an investment in and of itself—it's more like a savings account. Once money is put into a retirement account, most people invest it "through" the account into something like an index fund or other mutual fund.

These retirement accounts work well for most people who are slogging down the American Dream pathway, content with working until they are in their sixties or seventies. But *you*, my fellow FI Freak, are not most people. Your goal is to reach FI decades earlier, so these traditional retirement accounts may not be best for you.

When someone puts money into a retirement account, they generally cannot withdraw and use that money until around age 60. If they do take money out of their account before then, there can be a stiff penalty, and they may lose a sizable chunk of their money.

Therefore, one crucial benefit of putting your money into something *other* than retirement accounts is that you'll have easy access to it. Since you can easily access your money, you can later choose to invest it in other ways that will earn you passive income. You will need to depend on this money working for you *and* being available for withdrawal in order to reach early financial independence.

For example, having your money easily available would come in handy if one of your side hustles takes off and has a promising future. You may want to invest money into developing that opportunity. In this situation, having money in a retirement account will handicap the growth of that business because that money is unavailable for immediate withdrawal.

Let's take a quick look at retirement accounts that have penalties for early withdrawals:

- **401(k):** a workplace retirement account offered as an employee benefit and funded with your pretax income.
- **Traditional IRA:** a tax-favored retirement account funded with your pretax income.
- **Roth IRA:** Unlike traditional IRAs, Roth IRAs are funded with your *after*-tax dollars. Therefore, you can withdraw your contributions (but not your earnings) penalty-free.

Instead of investing your money in these types of accounts, I highly recommend putting your money to work elsewhere. You should use the next few years to invest your money in ways that can maximize your current potential and propel you down your FI pathway—and these retirement accounts will do neither.

More than 60 percent of Americans don't start saving for retirement (even with traditional retirement accounts) until age 30 or later. So even if you decide to start investing in these accounts a few years down the road, you will still be way ahead of most people. Besides, when you apply the Four Mechanisms and begin your journey to early FI, you are already saving for retirement, right *now*.

CHAPTER 24:
AN INTRODUCTION TO REAL ESTATE INVESTING

Ninety percent of all millionaires become so through owning real estate.

—ANDREW CARNEGIE, BILLIONAIRE INDUSTRIALIST

FREAK SPEAK

REI: Real estate investing.

Ninety percent is a massive number—big enough that anyone seeking early FI should pay attention.

Real estate investing is a vital, but sometimes complex, investment strategy. My goal here is to give you a high-level introduction to REI so you can have a basic understanding of this essential approach to building wealth. Don't get overwhelmed or intimidated by this concept just because it may be new and puzzling to you now. Digest the ideas in this chapter and know there is no immediate need to start your real estate investing career. You have *plenty* of time to learn and execute this valuable strategy.

Getting Started in REI

Set a goal to buy your first real estate property before turning 21. This is ambitious but doable. If your first purchase happens a year or two sooner or later, that's fine, but using REI as an investment tool will be crucial in your journey to early FI. If you shoot for age 21, you have the time between now and then to educate yourself, plan, and save. When the time comes, you will be more than prepared because you will have been Freakishly applying Mechanisms 1, 2, and 3.

Despite what you might think, investing in real estate is *not* difficult, and you don't have to be rich to do it. Many young people have used REI as an investment strategy with great success. You've met a few of them in the Featured Freak case studies throughout this book.

REI is very different from index fund investing. For one, REI is not as passive, which is its main drawback. REI involves more of your time than simply putting your money in an index fund and forgetting about it. However, REI is considered a passive income investment because the time commitment is far less than that required for other ways of earning money, like working a full-time job. Plus, when you own an investment property and have a tenant paying you rent, you earn money 24/7; that is where passive income comes in.

However, REI has several advantages that will more than make up for your increased time commitment—advantages like leverage, multiple wealth-building elements, property appreciation, and generational wealth. We'll explore each of these benefits in more detail. For now, just keep an open mind.

Another difference between index fund investing and REI is control. With the stock market, you have very little control because the companies you are invested in will not be asking for your input on important business decisions. With REI, you have massive control. *You* decide whether to buy a property and what type of property it will be. You'll also have to make decisions about who to accept as a tenant, how much rent to charge them, whether to make improvements to your property, and who, if anyone, you will hire to help you maintain, repair, and manage the property.

Four Things You Will Need to Do

1. Have an Income History

If you purchase real estate, you will probably have to get a mortgage. Before a lender agrees to loan you money, they will want to see that you have a steady income stream so you can make the monthly payments to repay the loan. The lender will verify this by reviewing your pay stubs and your annual tax returns.

Of the four items on this list, this is the biggest roadblock to buying your first property. If you decide not to go to college and instead begin full-time employment after high school, you should be able to get a mortgage by age 21 by following the steps in the FI Freak Checklist. If you decide to go to college after high school, building an income history sufficient to buy your first property by age 21 will be challenging, but it *is* possible. If you look for a property in a market where homes are generally of low value and you have had some ongoing part-time work, you may still qualify.

If you don't have enough of an income history when it comes time to buy your first property, you can have a co-signer or a co-borrower sign with you on the mortgage.

MORTGAGE: A legal agreement between a creditor and a borrower whereby the creditor loans the borrower money to purchase a property.

CO-SIGNER AND CO-BORROWER: Someone who signs a mortgage with a real estate buyer when the buyer does not have a sufficient income history or credit score. The income history of the co-signer or co-borrower can satisfy the lender's income requirements. Co-signers don't co-own the property, while co-borrowers do.

Having someone else sign the mortgage with you will allow you to buy that first property *if* you have taken care of items 3 and 4 on this list, which we'll get to in a moment. The co-signer or co-borrower will be responsible for making the mortgage payments in the event you are unable to do so.

Action to take: Get a W-2 job (part-time or full-time) and work consistently to build up a reliable income history.

 W-2 JOB: A job in which the hired person is considered an employee, not a contractor or self-employed. Most importantly, taxes are deducted from their wages and paid to the state and federal governments on their behalf. W-2 employees are called that because they receive a W-2 form at the end of the year to use in filing taxes.

In the eyes of a lender, W-2 jobs provide you with more reliable income. Typically, any job that requires you to fill out an application is a W-2 job.

2. Build Your Credit Score
Also important to the lender are your credit score and credit history. Now that you've read Chapter Eleven (Credit Score) and Chapter Twelve (Credit Cards), you know how to build a solid credit score. The FI Freak Checklist will walk you through the steps to get your first credit card and other ways to build your credit score. If you apply the principles in these chapters, a low or insufficient credit score should not be an issue for you—but you may have to use a co-signer or co-borrower, as described earlier.

Action to take: At age 18 (or as soon as you can if you are older than 18), get a credit card. At age 19, get a second credit card. In another six months, get a third credit card. Use all the credit cards responsibly and consistently while *always* paying off the balance each month.

3. Learn
I would not suggest you buy a property without first learning as much as you can about REI and the appropriate strategies, and there is a *lot* to learn. Lucky for you, you have plenty of time!

Between now and when you buy your first property, you will need to become familiar with REI by doing the following:
- Reading books
- Reading blogs
- Listening to podcasts

- Talking to other investors
- Finding a mentor
- Analyzing properties

By far the best place I know to learn about REI is BiggerPockets. It is the largest online community of real estate investors out there, with well over two million members, most of whom are willing to lend advice or help out a young aspiring investor on the blog or in the forums. BiggerPockets also publishes books—such as the one you're reading right now—on real estate investing, covering a range of material from flipping houses to managing rental properties.

Another great resource is YouTube, which has thousands of videos on just about every conceivable real estate–related topic.

Action to take: Spend an hour or two every week learning about REI.

4. Save

The last thing you will need for your first purchase is cold, hard cash for the down payment. Hello, Mechanism 3! As you already know, the more you hammer Mechanisms 1 and 2, the faster you will save money to invest.

How much will you need to buy a property? That's tough to answer because every geographical market is different. For example, Seattle, Washington, has very high prices for real estate, but a small city in the Midwest—like Cedar Rapids, Iowa—will have much lower prices.

Here's one example, just to give you a general idea. Let's say you are going to buy a house for $200,000. You are planning on house hacking this property, and since you will be living in the house, you'll need to make a 5 percent down payment. (By the way, even lower down payments are possible.) It's also wise to have $10,000 or so of backup money in case something breaks or goes wrong. So:

$200,000 × .05 = $10,000
Backup money = $10,000
Total needed = $20,000

Action to take: Perhaps start a side hustle in addition to your W-2 job. Practice frugality. Save a lot.

CHAPTER 25:
THE PROS AND CONS OF REAL ESTATE INVESTING

Real estate investing and the wealth it built have given me control over my life.

—CHAD CARSON, *RETIRE EARLY WITH REAL ESTATE*
@COACHCARSON1 @COACHCARSON1

Stock market investing, including index fund investing, has two main benefits: asset appreciation (the value going up over time) and dividend payouts. Real estate, on the other hand, has the benefit of *four* wealth generators. Let's take a quick look at the four ways REI can build your wealth.

Wealth Builder No. 1: Cash Flow
This is the extra income you receive each month. For example, if your tenant pays you $1,000 a month in rent and your total expenses for owning and managing the property are $800 a month, you will have a $200 monthly cash flow.

Wealth Builder No. 2: Appreciation

When the value of a property goes up, that's called appreciation. While appreciation is not guaranteed, real estate values have historically increased over time. For example, if you buy a property for $100,000 and ten years later it's worth $160,000, the property has appreciated by $60,000 (and your net worth has effectively increased by $60,000).

Wealth Builder No. 3: Loan Paydown

Every month that you make a mortgage payment on your property, the amount of money you owe the lender (your balance) decreases. However, when we talked about cash flow, we said all the expenses (including the mortgage payments) were more than covered by the tenant's rent payment. This means that over time, *your tenant* is paying the loan down for you, helping you build wealth.

For example, let's say you buy a property for $200,000 and put 5 percent ($10,000) down. The mortgage amount would be $190,000. You then make your monthly mortgage payments to the lender using the money you get from the tenant's rent payments.

After thirty years (the usual length of a mortgage), the mortgage will be paid off and you will owe $0 to the lender. Even if we assume that there's been zero appreciation over those thirty years (which is highly unlikely), you now completely own an asset valued at $200,000, and you paid only $10,000 at the beginning! Because your tenant's rent paid the mortgage for you, they built *your* wealth. This is why we say mortgages for rental properties are good debt, as we discussed in Chapter Ten.

Wealth Builder No. 4: Tax Benefits

The U.S. government wants to encourage investors to buy properties and provide safe, affordable housing for its citizens. The tax system is designed to encourage people to invest in real estate. Because of these tax incentives, real estate investors can pay *significantly* less in taxes than other business owners. Paying less tax to the government means you keep more of your money and build wealth faster.

Other Reasons to Invest in Real Estate

My biggest money mistake is that I didn't invest in real estate soon enough.

—GRANT SABATIER ON THE *BIGGERPOCKETS MONEY PODCAST*, EPISODE 58
◎ @MILLENNIALMONEYCOM

Control

As a teenager, I'm sure you know how frustrating it is to not have maximum control over your life since your parents still call most of the shots. Think of your investments in the same way. Would you rather call the shots or let others have control of your money?

When it comes to real estate, you have a great deal of control over your investments. And when it comes to reaching your financial goals, having control of your investments can be a very good thing.

With a rental property, you call the shots. Some factors, like the overall real estate market, are beyond your control, but most are not. *You* decide which type of rental property to buy, how thoroughly to analyze a property before you buy it, how long to own it, which investment strategy to use, how to choose your tenants, how much to spend on improving the property, who to hire to help you with repairs, and more.

Availability of Free Information

Although it may not seem that way now, REI is not complicated—but there is still a fair amount you'll need to know before making your first purchase. Luckily, lots of helpful information is available for free or at a very low cost. Thousands of others have gone down the path of REI, and many will be happy to share their experiences and wisdom with you.

There are thousands of books and articles about REI, many of them aimed at beginners. You can also take advantage of hundreds of free REI podcasts and YouTube videos.

Now pay attention to this next part, as it is extremely important. (And yes, I know I say that a lot—but only because it all really is important!) Many people will try to tell you they have the secret to easy and fast income from REI. *Run from those people as fast as you can!* Usually, after a free introductory seminar or workshop, they will try to sell you their "full" system for hundreds or thousands of dollars. *Don't fall for it.* Everything they are trying to sell you is available for free or less than $20.

Passive Income

Many people consider real estate to be the best passive income investment there is. While index fund investing is technically more passive than REI, it doesn't offer as many benefits.

For sure, REI requires *some* work. But once you start enjoying the benefits of REI's four wealth builders, you will find yourself "sold" on real estate investing as the best way to build wealth.

Your first property is always the toughest to purchase. Buying your second will be way easier, with fewer mistakes and no first-time jitters. Your third will be a piece of cake—at which point, you'll be off and running down the Freak freeway to FI!

Leverage

Leverage is one of REI's most valuable tools because it maximizes your money's potential.

To understand how, let's start by looking at index fund investing. If you want to own $10,000 of an S&P 500 index fund, you have to save up and invest $10,000.

Real estate, however, is different. You can invest in a property for only a fraction of its total worth. For example, to buy a $200,000 house, you have to save up only $10,000 for a 5 percent down payment, which is possible with some REI strategies.

Even though you invested just $10,000 of your own money, you are getting the full benefit of a $200,000 investment, minus the interest you are paying on the mortgage. You are leveraging $10,000 of your hard-earned, hard-saved money into a much larger investment. If not for leverage, you would have to save up $200,000 to benefit from a $200,000 investment.

FREAK SPEAK

LEVERAGE: The use of borrowed money to increase the potential return of an investment. The goal is to earn a return greater than the interest you paid to borrow the money.

Leverage gives you the power to make more money by using someone else's money (usually, a lender's or a bank's) at the same time as your own. It's a tool that can be very helpful in growing your wealth and getting you to FI. However, it can also work against you, which is important to keep in mind. We will talk about that at the end of this chapter.

Forced Appreciation
Welcome to one of the best strategies in REI! Forced appreciation takes work, but I know you're up for it. This strategy will bring you thousands of dollars of equity, wealth, and additional rent over your REI career. Buckle up, take notes, and smile, because you're about to learn a strategy most REI investors pass up.

 EQUITY: The total value you have in an investment. Equity equals the current value of an investment minus the amount you owe on that investment.

If you own a rental property valued at $200,000 but you owe $150,000 to the lender, your equity is $50,000. That's how much money you would have left after paying off the mortgage if you sold the property. Therefore, when a property's value increases, your equity in the property also increases. This is why any kind of appreciation (aka, increase in value) is important.

Market appreciation happens when a property increases in value over time simply because of an increase in the local real estate market. Investors have little control over this. Forced appreciation, on the other hand, happens when the owner does something that increases the value of the property *regardless* of what the local real estate market is doing. By forcing appreciation, the owner increases their equity.

Let's say you buy an older house in a great neighborhood. Your new house needs some work both inside and out, so you do some research and learn which upgrades and improvements make the most sense. You spend $25,000 on some strategically chosen changes, such as building a new front porch, painting the garage, redoing the bathroom tile, and buying new appliances for the kitchen. If the $25,000 you spend on upgrades and repairs increases the value of the house by $55,000, the

$30,000 difference is the forced appreciation.

 FORCED APPRECIATION: An increase in the value of a property due to investor actions such as improvements, upgrades, or additions.

Another way to force appreciation is to add utility or space to the property. Let's say you buy a house that is in excellent condition (no repairs needed). The house has two bedrooms, one bathroom, and a sunroom. Because people value bedrooms and bathrooms more than add-ons like dens, sunrooms, and screened-in porches, you could pay someone to change that sunroom into a bedroom and almost certainly add value to the property. If it costs you $10,000 to turn the sunroom into a bedroom and doing so increases the value of the property by $25,000, you've just "forced" $15,000 in appreciation.

However you go about it, using forced appreciation can increase your equity in the property and therefore increase your net worth. But there's yet another benefit: The things you do to force appreciation also make the property nicer to live in, which means you can charge higher rent. And higher rent increases your monthly cash flow from the property!

Generational Wealth

 GENERATIONAL WEALTH: Wealth that is passed down from one generation to the next.

REI is a strategy that will help you leave a legacy by passing on your real estate investments to your heirs. Let's dig into this concept by once again comparing REI to index fund investing.

If you invest in index funds (as you should) and start sustainable asset withdrawals later in life after reaching FI, you will be spending the money you've invested. The 4 Percent Rule allows you to live off your investments until you die, but you will still *use* most or all of the money during the retirement phase of life. In other words, there will be little or no money left to pass on to your children or grandchildren.

Real estate is entirely different. If you have ten rental properties when you die, those properties don't die with you—they can get passed on to your heirs. That means your heirs would get not just the properties but also the equity, the monthly cash flow, and the tax benefits of each. With REI, you are setting up a substantial inheritance for your heirs. Maybe *you* could be the first one in your family to start a legacy of generational wealth.

In their research, authors Thomas J. Stanley and William D. Danko of *The Millionaire Next Door* found that most of America's millionaires are first-generation rich. What does that mean for you? It means that no matter what your current situation is and how much wealth your family does or does not have right now, you have every opportunity to accumulate $1 million or more of wealth. As the authors say, "America continues to hold great prospects for those who wish to accumulate wealth in one generation."

The Cons of REI

Investing in real estate is not for everybody, and like every type of investment, it does have its drawbacks. Although I am *strongly* in favor of young people getting involved in REI at an early age as a long-term investing strategy, I wouldn't be doing my job if I didn't tell you about the downsides. You should take these cons seriously, but also know that all real estate investors face these same disadvantages, and thousands upon thousands of real estate investors are extremely successful anyway.

Market Downturns

The risk of investing in the stock market is that the value of your investments could go down. The same is true for real estate because the value of your property can go down.

If this does happen, it's likely not just your property that's affected but the entire neighborhood, city, state, or country. In 2008, real estate values across the United States took a dive because of widespread financial issues. Property values can also decrease for reasons that are strictly local. For example, if a major employer in the town where you are investing goes bankrupt and hundreds of people lose their jobs, real estate values could take a hit.

It's impossible to predict what real estate values will do in the short term, just as it is impossible to predict whether stocks will go up or down. Still, history indicates that real estate values generally go up over the long term, just like index funds and the stock market.

Leverage

As we already discussed, leverage allows you to maximize your returns. But if there's a market downturn, leverage can also work against you.

For example, I once bought a property for $150,000. After the down payment, my mortgage was for $140,000. Then the real estate crisis of 2008 hit, and after a year or two, the property was worth only $100,000. This meant that if I wanted to sell the property, I would have had to *pay* $40,000 just to get rid of it! That's because I would have needed to pay off the mortgage of $140,000 (minus the amount of the loan I had paid since the purchase, which wasn't much). Since I would have received only $100,000 from the sale, I would have had to come up with another $40,000 to pay off the mortgage.

Lucky for me, I was in it for the long haul. I held on to the property and continued to rent it out. About seven years later, the property's value had not only rebounded, but gone up quite a bit—I sold it for $175,000.

Each property you buy using borrowed money puts you deeper in debt. As we've said before, mortgages on investment properties are considered "good" debt. However, if the real estate market in your area were to take a drastic turn for the worse, it could be extremely difficult to keep up with your debt if your properties decrease in value and/or the amount of rent you can get from tenants goes down.

REI Wealth Doesn't Happen Overnight

All of your investments should be for the long term, and real estate is no different. REI is not a get-rich-quick plan. Many will say it is, but they are likely trying to scam you into buying something from them. (Remember, *run away* from these people!) REI is an investment strategy you should use for the rest of your life. If you do, you will build massive amounts of wealth.

Real Estate Is Not a Liquid Asset

Many other investments are highly "liquid," meaning you can convert them to cash quickly. Real estate, however, is not liquid because properties can't be sold instantly. Real estate investors must be prepared to own a property for years, and during that time, they will not be able to use the money they have invested in the property for other purposes.

It's Not 100 Percent Passive

When you do buy your first property, I highly recommend you manage it yourself. You could pay someone to manage it for you, but you would miss out on all the learning opportunities that come with self-managing.

Managing your property will become a part-time job. You will spend time communicating with tenants and maintenance people. You will need to find new tenants when old ones move out. You will have to stay on top of maintenance and repairs. These things are time-consuming, but they are all great learning experiences. (Plus, you will save money by not paying someone else to manage your property.)

REI does take time, but it's time well spent. Just know going into it that you will be adding some responsibilities to your plate.

Other People Aren't Always Reliable

Even if you follow the best tips and advice for finding great tenants, you may still end up with a bad one. This could be someone who doesn't pay rent, doesn't follow the lease's rules, or damages your property. There are ways to deal with bad tenants, but none of them are fun. The risk of getting a bad tenant is one downside to REI. The best plan is to have a well-thought-out system for screening prospective tenants *before* you let them move into your property. This reduces the risk significantly.

Beyond tenants, you may need to rely on other people to make repairs, mow the lawn, or remodel the kitchen. Just because *you* are loyal, honest, and hardworking doesn't mean all the people you hire to do work for you will be as well. There will be disagreements and disappointments.

Here's Brandon Turner's advice on how to best deal with other people in the real estate business:

> *You can limit your exposure to difficult people by managing effectively. By doing [the work] up front to find a great contractor or property manager, you will reduce the probability that you will later need to fire that person. By screening your tenants exceptionally well, you'll be able to weed out the ones who will cause you the most damage.*

You Will Need to Become a Bookkeeper

As you start to buy rental properties, you'll have to learn to keep track of the money and documents involved. After all, you will be bringing in income (rent) and paying expenses. You will also be dealing with leases, insurance, and multiple receipts. Keeping track of everything will help you get the best tax benefits, one of the four wealth builders of REI.

There's no need to feel overwhelmed, though. It's not like you're going to wake up one day owning five rental properties. You will buy them one at a time. While owning your first property, you will learn how to manage all the relevant paperwork and bookkeeping. Once you do, the good news is that staying on top of your records should only take about one or two hours a week. Between now and your first purchase, there is plenty of time to slowly learn what you need to know to handle this part of REI.

It Can Be Addictive

I'll admit, this is a bit of a facetious "con." Nonetheless, many real estate investors have a hard time containing their enthusiasm. Once they own a property or two and actually see the financial benefits of REI, they want to buy more and more. Sometimes they get carried away.

It can be hard not to get caught up in the "think big" mentality. But you don't have to own a hundred properties to be a success. Keep your goal of early FI in mind. Five properties might be all you need.

Of course, if you enjoy building your portfolio and managing all its components, there's nothing wrong with owning more. Just do so knowing you are creating a job for yourself, even though at the start the whole idea was to *not* have to work. Try to keep things as simple as possible while reaching your goal of early FI. Don't get caught up in other people's goals or what they say you should be doing.

The objective is not to be the person with the most properties—it's to have the freedom and flexibility to do the things on your happiness list.

REI Conclusion

There *are* drawbacks to REI, but none are impossible to overcome. Plus, you're probably years away from your first real estate purchase, so you have plenty of time to learn about anything you don't fully understand. Don't sell yourself short by avoiding REI. If you slowly educate yourself about REI over the next few years, you'll be more than ready to invest when the time comes.

The REI world offers many strategies and opportunities. For now, just be aware that REI has terrific benefits. Many millionaires have used REI to accumulate massive wealth. Those same advantages are there for you if you decide to use them.

Combining Index Funds and REI

As I mentioned earlier, these two main investing strategies for reaching early FI are very different. Because each has its pros and cons, the best approach is to use both in your pursuit of early FI.

As you start working on Mechanisms 1, 2, and 3, you will find yourself with more and more money accumulating in your future investment savings account. Congratulations! You will then need to decide how you will invest that money. You can choose how much will go toward index funds and how much will go to REI. Maybe you'll decide a 50/50 split is best for you, or maybe 40/60 or 75/25.

There is no right answer, and you don't need to decide right now. As long as you understand that *all* investments are long-term commitments, you will win, so don't sweat it. Instead, be excited and grateful that you have made it this far and therefore understand more about your money and investing than just about anyone else your age. You are definitely a FI Freak!

CODY BERMAN

@ @codydberman

Where do you currently live?
Leicester, Massachusetts.

How old are you? Twenty-four.

How old were you when you started actively pursuing financial independence? Nineteen.

What was your profession/career/job when you first started pursuing FI? I was working in commerical real estate lending.

Do you consider yourself financially independent today? How many years did it take you to reach FI?
Yes. Five years.

If you have reached FI, what job do you have now, if any?
I like to consider myself an experimental entrepreneur. I don't have a formal 9-to-5 job, but I do like to stay busy.

Who or what got you started on your FI path?
I started to get interested in finan-cial independence after reading *The 4-Hour Workweek* by Timothy Ferriss and realizing that money and time did not have to be linearly related. Instead, I could build businesses and create passive income streams now that would pay me dividends in perpetuity.

What is your Why of FI?
I don't want money to control my life. Unfortunately, so many people find themselves in a position where they "have" to work for that next paycheck in order to pay the bills, service their debt, or support their lifestyle. I like having the flexibility to travel, work on creative projects, and spend time on personal development.

What is or has been your favorite way to save money and why?
Since I started pursuing FI, I have always kept two expense categories as close to zero as possible: housing and transportation. I actually make money with house hacking, and I drive a paid-off car, which requires

a small insurance payment each month and general maintenance costs. It may not seem like I'm doing anything crazy (because I'm not), but these two things help me save tens of thousands of dollars each year.

What is or has been your favorite way to increase your income and why?

Building passive income streams is one of the best ways to hit financial independence as fast as possible. With my online courses and my real estate investments, I spent a considerable amount of time building them and putting all my systems in place. But now the businesses can practically run themselves with minimal effort on my end.

What is your current savings rate?

My savings rate is 80 to 90 percent, depending on the month.

If you invest in the stock market, what is your preferred type of investment or method?

Mutual funds.

How many real estate properties do you own? What types are they?

I own three properties myself and three jointly with my brother.

Have you ever house hacked? If so, explain.

Yes. My girlfriend and I lived in one unit of our triplex for several months, and now we live in the detached unit that's part of one of my properties.

What has been your biggest challenge in pursing FI and why?

When I explain what I'm doing to many friends and family members, they are in utter disbelief. The idea of FI or early retirement seems like a pipe dream. I've heard it all from "you have no idea what you're doing" to "oh no, that's impossible" to a dismissive "oh, nice."

Would you change anything about your path to FI? If so, what?

I wish I'd started investing in real estate a bit sooner.

What one piece of advice would you give a teenager who wants to achieve early FI?

Live like a young adult for as long as possible. For some reason, when many people get a taste of earning "real" money, their first temptation is to spend nearly all of it (or more). Resist this temptation with every bone in your body! If you don't fall victim to lifestyle inflation, you will have a massive advantage over your older adult counterparts. If you can earn a decent wage and resist these temptations from your late teens through your mid-twenties, it will be hard not to accumulate wealth!

If you are all in with your FI journey, then it's time to remind everyone that you're a FI Freak. Take a photo of yourself with the next two pages open and post it on all your social media with the hashtags **#ALLINFREAK** and **#TEENAGEFIFREAK.**

Don't forget to tag **@BIGGERPOCKETS** and **@SHEEKSFREAKS!**

FI
FREAK

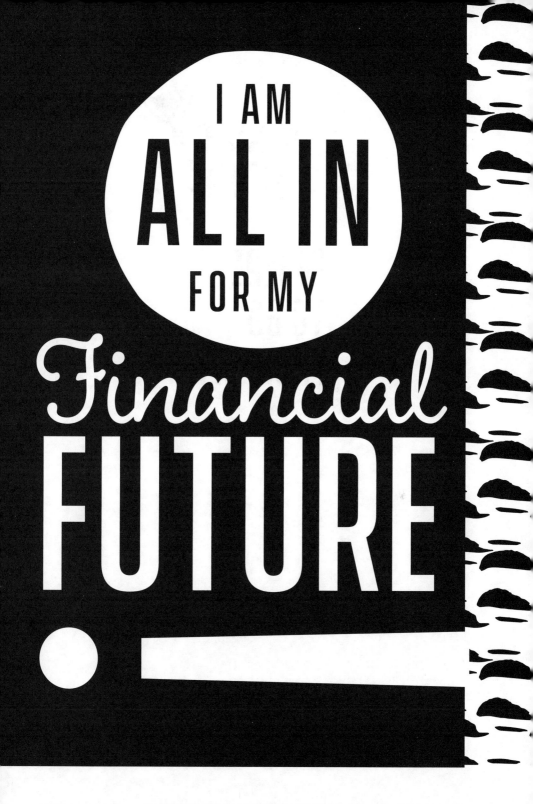

I AM ALL IN FOR MY *Financial* FUTURE

PART SIX

WHERE TO GO FROM HERE

Just get started. For a lot of folks, that probably means just get started learning more and educating yourself, and starting to feel confident . . . You really don't have to know all the nitty-gritty, all of the complicated stuff. You can keep it pretty simple. But you do have to have a basic understanding in order to just feel confident in yourself. And you are completely capable of doing this!

—ERIN LOWRY ON THE *BIGGERPOCKETS MONEY PODCAST*, EPISODE 81

The final section of this book will guide you in making some tough decisions going forward. Chapters Twenty-Six and Twenty-Seven will tackle the often-controversial college question. Should you go? And if you do, what's the best strategy for getting your degree without giving up your early FI goals?

In Chapter Twenty-Eight, we'll look at the pros and cons of being a teenager on a pathway to early FI. (Spoiler alert: There are many more pros than cons!) We'll close the book with Chapter Twenty-Nine, where I'll explain the other resource you can use to continue your FI Freak journey: the FI Freak Checklist.

CHAPTER 26:
SHOULD YOU GO TO COLLEGE?

Education is great. We've all seen the studies about how much more money people make over the course of their careers when they go to college, grad school, or become doctors and lawyers. I'm not here to argue with that. It is absolutely true that over the course of a forty-year career, you will likely earn way more money with higher education. **But only if you have a forty-year career.**

—SCOTT TRENCH, "3 NEGATIVELY CASH-FLOWING 'ASSETS' THAT CAN DEVASTATE YOUR FINANCES," BIGGERPOCKETS BLOG
@SCOTT_TRENCH

As I set out to write this book, I knew this chapter would be the hardest to put together. Whether or not to go to college is one of the most significant decisions we examine in this book. It is also one of the most emotional and, at times, controversial choices you will face. (For simplicity's sake, whenever I use the word "college," I am also referring to universities.)

For some of you, going to college is not in the cards. Maybe that's because your grades aren't adequate, it's not an expectation for you, or it's not possible financially. I think you may actually have an advantage because your choice is already made—and skipping college does *not* mean you won't succeed!

For others, going to college is a given. This may be because you have a parent who expects you to do so. They may have worked very hard to save money for this to be your reality. Or it could be that *you* have made up your mind you will go to college to pursue a dream or passion.

There is a third category: the undecided. If you fall into this category, you are likely the one who will choose whether or not to go to college. However you choose, your decision will affect your financial future for decades—and you are being asked to make this *enormous* decision at the age of 17 or 18.

Okay, should you go to college or not? You've been patiently waiting for my answer, and here it is: *I have no freaking idea.*

I cannot tell anyone, and certainly not a group of readers I've never met, what their choice should be. It depends on so many variables and personal circumstances, and even when you take all of those into consideration, the answer is sometimes still not clear. Bottom line: There is no right or wrong answer. Either decision can lead to success or failure—it all depends on how you proceed once you've made the choice.

In this chapter, we will examine the pros and cons of both options, as well as some alternatives. I hope to provide enough information for you to be confident in your choice, no matter what it may be.

Consider This First

This book is about reaching early financial independence. For most people, the main reason for hustling so hard to reach FI is so they won't have to work anymore. Early FI will give them the freedom to spend their time how they want. Their goal is to allocate most of their time to the things that bring them the most happiness and to work toward their Why of FI.

Before we ponder the question of whether college is the right choice for you, let's take a step back and look at the big picture. Only when we do this can we see the overall need for or value of a college degree.

One thing is certain: You will have to work. A full-time job will create a steady income that will allow your Four Mechanisms to start working. When I talk about Mechanism 1, *earn more*, I'm talking about the idea of generating income above and beyond your full-time job with a part-time gig or a side hustle. Therefore, a full-time job is the foundation for your earning potential and is paramount to the early FI journey.

If your goal is to reach early FI and then quit whatever job helped get you there, you should seriously consider just how necessary it is to spend four years and thousands of dollars to land a job you may have for less than ten years. So the question becomes, "What job do I want to have while pursuing FI?"

If you skip college and start working full-time right after high school, you can begin hammering the Four Mechanisms years sooner than if you go to college. There are many jobs that do not require a college degree but can still adequately fund your early FI pursuit. On the other hand, if you do go to college, you will likely land a higher-paying job. That higher income will help you save and invest more, but it will happen four years later. Going to college can also leave you with massive student loan debt that can offset that higher income. What's the answer? Again, it's a personal choice *you* must make.

Know What You Want to Do

Some young people know what full-time job or profession they want to have. Maybe they've always dreamed of being a teacher, and they are all but certain a job in education will be rewarding and joyful. If you want to pursue a job that requires a college degree, such as teaching, I am 90 percent certain you should go to college. (I'm rarely 100 percent certain of anything.)

But what if you have no idea what you want to do for that full-time job you'll need? Based on the 1,000-plus high schoolers I've had the pleasure of knowing over my career, most teens are right there with you. It's difficult to know what you want to do for a career at such an early age, whether you're a FI Freak or not. Don't let the not-knowing stress you out. If you're not sure or have no idea at all, that is perfectly fine and normal.

When making this decision, you first need to ask yourself a fundamental question: "Why would I go to college?" That may seem ridiculously simple and obvious, but don't take it lightly. If your answer is, "I've always wanted to be a lawyer, and I need a degree to do that," then go. However, if your answer is one of the following, you may want to reconsider going to college:

- I want to go to college because my parents say I should (or must).
- I want to go to college because all my friends are going.
- I want to go to college because smart people go to college and dumb people don't.
- I want to go to college because it guarantees that I will make a lot of money, and that's worth it, no matter how much student loan debt I rack up in the process.
- I want to go to college to have fun and party.
- I want to go to college to figure out what I want to do with my life while I'm there.
- I want to go to college to get away from my hometown/parents/friends.

Going to college for one of these reasons can be a costly and massive mistake. Take it from someone who knows.

The Short Version of My Story

As I was nearing the end of high school, I had no idea what I wanted to do for a career. But I did know one thing: I wanted to be rich. I grew up in a lower-middle-class, single-parent family, and we lived on a strict budget. That experience made one thing clear to me—I did not want money to be a constant source of stress in my life. Therefore, I needed to become rich, and the American Dream told me (and everyone else) that going to college was the best way to accomplish that.

My mother really hoped I would head to college after high school because she wanted what was best for me. She wanted me to have a successful future, and a four-year degree was the path to get there. Together, we decided I would go to college.

Although my family had little money, I decided to go to an expensive private college. I received many scholarships and grants, but they weren't nearly enough to cover the total costs. Student loans became part of my financial package to pay for college.

Little did I know that I would be burdened with student loan debt for *decades* to come, and those loans would prevent me from finding financial freedom until they were completely paid off. Nobody ever told me the effect student loans would have on my life after graduating with that college degree. To be honest, if I had known about the repercussions, I might have decided against college. Or, at the very least, I would have chosen a much more affordable school.

Since I had absolutely no idea what I wanted to do, I decided to major in business. That made sense to me because, again, I wanted to be rich. Businesspeople don't have money problems, right? Once I got to college, I met friends majoring in education, music, and psychology. I often made lighthearted fun of them: "Why would you choose a career that paid so little money?" Little did I know how *my* life would play out.

I graduated from college with a degree in business and a massive amount of student loan debt. I didn't feel like starting my forty-year career right away (mostly because I *still* didn't know what kind of job I wanted). Instead, I decided to travel and took a series of short-term seasonal jobs, from snowmaker in Vermont to bartender in St. Thomas to housekeeper in the Rocky Mountains. I was having fun and seeing the world, but I was also dreading a full-time job. In fact, I was starting to doubt whether I even wanted a business career.

Fast-forward a few years, and I'm 27 years old. This was when I decided to become a high school teacher—the same profession some of my college friends had chosen when I was making fun of them! Back to college I went to get my teaching license. After two years of additional college classes (and even *more* student loan debt), I landed my first teaching job at age 29. I've now been teaching high school business classes for about twenty years.

There are three main points I hope you take away from my story:

1. I didn't know what I wanted to do with my life when I graduated from high school, and it's okay if you don't either.
2. Committing to four years of school and tens of thousands of dollars of debt when I had no idea what I wanted to do was a mistake. I should have waited.
3. Student loans handicapped my financial life for *decades*. (A few years after I started teaching, I got a master's degree and acquired even *more* student loan debt!)

Exploring Your Passion

There are two uncommon scenarios in which obtaining a [college degree] makes sense. The first is if you can obtain a free education. The second is if you are truly passionate about the work done in a field where an education is needed (such as a doctor, lawyer, etc.).

—CRAIG CURELOP, "5 ROADBLOCKS ON THE PATH TOWARD FINANCIAL FREEDOM,"
BIGGERPOCKETS BLOG
@THEFIGUY @THEFIGUY

I would never tell anyone not to explore their passion or pursue their dreams—but if your passion does require a college degree, make sure it is indeed a passion and not just an interest. You should *not* go to college just to explore an interest; there are much more affordable ways to do so. Don't mistake an interest for a passion.

For example, if animals are interesting to you, that is not a legitimate reason to go to school to be a veterinarian. You could satisfy your interest in many other ways, such as being a foster parent for shelter animals, volunteering at a zoo, or getting a side hustle walking dogs. However, if you are so *passionate* about animals that you cannot imagine your life without them, you can see yourself enjoying focusing on animals all day for five days a week, and you are willing to dedicate the next two or three decades of your life to becoming one of the leading experts on animals in your area, then you have a *passion*, not just an interest.

Be honest about what is and is not a passion for you. Your favorite subject in school or the subject you are best at is not always a passion. At your young age, you may not yet know what your passion is. It may take a few more years of getting to know yourself and exploring outside your comfort zone to discover your passion. Not to make it even more unnerving, but your passion can change over time, sometimes drastically.

If you are about to spend four years (or more) of time and money pursuing a passion, do yourself a huge favor and make absolutely sure it's not just an interest.

The Trade-Off

Essentially, your decision hinges on one significant trade-off: You can either have a full-time focus on earning and investing money right away, or you can wait to do so with the higher income you'll earn once you get a college degree.

On one end of the trade-off is the decision to graduate from high school and start earning money by working full-time right away or within a couple of years. It would involve maximizing the Four Mechanisms as best you can right out of the gate. The aim is to earn as much as you can, spend less by living frugally, save the difference, and invest it wisely.

On the other end of the trade-off is the decision to go to college, which requires time and money. Over those four (or so) years, you are deciding to trade that time and money for the ability to make a higher income once you graduate. While going to school, you can still work the Four Mechanisms but in a limited capacity. However, once you have the degree, you can really start to hammer them with a higher income (we hope) than you would have had if you had not gone to college.

Since none of us can see into the future, we will never know which option is best for you. Once you've made your choice, you just need to move forward with it and use this book's strategies to reach early FI with your chosen journey.

Why You Shouldn't Go

Am I saying that education isn't important? Not at all. Education is the foundation of success. I'm saying that school is just one place to learn.

—ROBERT KIYOSAKI, *RICH DAD POOR DAD FOR TEENS*
@THEREALKIYOSAKI THE RICH DAD CHANNEL

You Don't Know What You Want to Do

As we discussed earlier, paying a ton of money and spending a lot of time to study something you may or may not want to pursue as a career is the opposite of Freakish—it's foolish. The college "road" has too high a toll if it's taking you somewhere you may not want to go. You need to ask yourself, "Is college necessary for me to reach my goals?"

If you're still figuring out what type of full-time job you want to do, consider taking a gap year after high school. I've seen a dramatic increase in the number of my seniors who choose this excellent option.

There are several advantages to taking a gap year:

- You can explore a field to see if you enjoy it first.
- You can travel and do service work.
- You can make and save some money by working.
- You can probably continue to live with your parents to keep your expenses low.
- You can always start college a year later with the new incoming freshman class.

FREAK SPEAK

FS

GAP YEAR: A period, typically an academic year, taken by a student as a break between high school and higher education in order to explore professional and personal opportunities.

Waiting one year to figure out if college is right for you could pay off enormously. The growth and awareness that result from spending a year doing service work in a foreign country, traveling the world, or beginning your journey to FI to see if you like it can be extraordinary.

Whether or not you take a gap year, if you are unsure about why you would go to college, there's one thing you should *not* do: go to college, rack up loads of student loan debt, and end up with a degree for a profession you have little interest in, all while losing four years of precious time when you could have been striving toward early FI.

Opportunity Cost

If you go to college and you graduate in four years with $100,000 in debt with a degree in history, you're not in a very strong position. The fella that [didn't go to college] is likely much

*farther along and is much more likely to achieve
financial independence much sooner than you.*

—SCOTT TRENCH, *BIGGERPOCKETS MONEY PODCAST*, EPISODE 126

@ @SCOTT_TRENCH

FS **OPPORTUNITY COST:** The lost benefit of possible gains from other options when one option is chosen.

Another reason for not going to college is because you would be giving up the benefits another alternative offers. For example, you might be forfeiting the experiences you would have during a gap year, or missing out on the wealth you would acquire if you invested your tuition money over those four years.

Here's another scenario, albeit an extreme one.

Some of your high school friends may be headed to high-status jobs as lawyers or doctors. (There is nothing wrong with that if that's what they *know* they want to do.) Let's look at a doctor's educational path: They will attend four years of college. From there, they will attend medical school for another four years. After that, they will have a residency (working in a medical facility as an intern) for three to seven years. This means the earliest they will begin "working" their first job is age 29, *and* they will likely have racked up massive student loan debt in the process.

Meanwhile, you decided to skip college. Instead, you started working right after graduating from high school. You got a full-time job, plus you started putting time and energy into a side hustle, earning even more. You lived frugally while not skimping on things you value. After a year, you started investing in index funds. A year later, you bought your first real estate investment property. Fast-forward a few years, and you'll have reached financial independence at the exact same time your doctor friend finishes their residency and *begins* their career.

Some might say, "Yeah, but the doctor will be able to help people for years, which will be very rewarding and fulfilling, not to mention good for society." Great point. But so can the person who has reached FI! They can also help numerous people for years after they reach FI, and they can do so in many ways. They could join the Peace Corps, volunteer at an orphanage or children's hospital, help build or renovate a neighborhood park, help teach elementary school students to read, work for minimum wage at a pet shelter . . . or they could choose to do *all* these things. That's because they would have the freedom of time. Someone who has achieved FI can give back and help others in whatever way they want.

Once again, if you have always wanted to be a medical doctor and it's truly your passion, go for it. Just become comfortable with the opportunity cost first.

Save the Money

If you're considering investing in a college education, think twice before accumulating that bad debt. Those are years you won't get back. Money is often spent on irrelevant information, and those loans will keep taking money out of your pocket for years.

—STERLING WHITE, "THE NO. 1 REASON YOU'RE BROKE (& HOW TO CHANGE YOUR FATE)," BIGGERPOCKETS BLOG

@STERLINGWHITEOFFICIAL   STERLING WHITE

Um, college is expensive. Tuition, room, board, books, and fees add up quickly, and it's generally a pretty significant number. Most high school seniors going to college don't realize how significant that number is. They don't take the time to let that number sink in. According to Educationdata. org, the total of *all* expenses for four years at an in-state public school is more than $100,000.

Maybe your parents have saved a lot of money for your college expenses. Maybe you are receiving a healthy amount of grants and scholarships. If so, great! But unless those cover *everything*, you still should look at the bottom line. If your parents' savings plus your scholarships and grants will pay for half of that $100,000, *you're still responsible for $50,000.* And that's not counting the opportunity cost of the money you could have earned were you not in school full-time. Just keep this in mind when making your decision. What else could that money be doing?

For example, let's say your parents have $50,000 saved for college. What if you decided not to go? Instead, you ask your parents to give you half the money (they can keep the other half for themselves), which you then use to start your own business or buy your first real estate investment property. You just saved $50,000 in student loan debt, received $25,000 in seed money for an investment, and freed up four years of your life during which you can earn even more money to invest!

You Don't Need a College Degree to Get a Good Job

I think colleges are basically for fun and to prove you can do your chores, but they're not for learning.

—ELON MUSK

Many high-paying jobs do not require a four-year degree. You might need a year or two of education, apprenticeship, or vocational training to secure one of these jobs, but you won't have to devote four years of time and tuition to get them. Here are just a few:

- Media and communications equipment worker
- Electronics repairer
- Commercial pilot
- Aircraft mechanic
- Court reporter
- Merchant marine
- Wind turbine technician
- Tool and die maker
- Firefighter
- HVAC and refrigeration technician
- Broadcast and sound technician
- Real estate broker
- Radiation therapist
- Patrol officer
- Sales representative

- Certified plumber
- Certified electrician
- Structural iron and steelworker
- Bus driver
- Licensed vocational nurse
- Sheet metal worker

In addition, some major ccorporations—including IBM, Google, Apple, Costco Wholesale, and Bank of America—are starting to relax their requirement that new hires have a bachelor's degree. These well-known, established companies realize that a motivated high school graduate can be a better long-term employee than an "educated" recruit fresh out of college.

Also, keep this in mind: The whole purpose of this book and the FI Freak Checklist is for you to reach financial independence *early* in life. In doing so, you will have the option not to work or to work however you want. Think about whether getting a college degree even matters to you. If you go to college to earn a degree and then reach FI after a few years, do you think you would leave the job that required a degree? If so, is it worth four years of time and tuition for the five to ten years of using that degree for the job you no longer want? Maybe. Maybe not.

Why You Should Go

The function of education is to teach one to think intensively and to think critically. Intelligence plus character—that is the goal of true education.

—DR. MARTIN LUTHER KING JR., "THE PURPOSE OF EDUCATION"

Education

Obviously, the number one reason for going to college is to learn. But let's be brutally honest for a minute: If a college student isn't excited and motivated to learn, they won't.

You know this better than anyone. Think of that math or science class you loathe going to every day. You have zero motivation to learn the material (except to get a good grade). College is no different. If you don't have the self-motivation to go to class, study, and learn, isn't it a waste of time and money?

However, if you *do* have a burning desire to learn and explore your chosen field, college can be a fantastic launching pad for your future. If you are focused and determined to learn all you can while you're there, then every penny and hour spent on acquiring your college degree will be worth it.

A Higher-Income Job

Spending four years of time and tuition to get a degree that will not deliver a solid return on your investment is a bad idea. It is also a bad idea to go to college only to make the same amount of money you would have made if you had not gone. Even worse is choosing a major that will make it extremely difficult to find a job at all.

However, if you choose the right major and get a degree that can earn you double or even triple the amount you would have been making without it, that's a good investment. Suppose you earn a higher income for five to ten years. In that case, the additional amount you earn can minimize or even eliminate the financial and opportunity cost of going to college.

Better still is choosing a major that leads to a job you decide to stick with even after reaching FI. Maybe you earn your four-year degree and get your dream job as an architect. You then reach early FI but choose to keep working just because you love it. If so, you'll have increased the return on your college investment even more.

Other Advantages

Going to college can provide benefits beyond the academic. You shouldn't underestimate the value of the college experience as a whole. When I talk about my college experience with my students, I tell them it was one of the best times of my life. I had few responsibilities, new and numerous freedoms, and dozens of friends who lived within a five-minute walk.

A major benefit of going to college is the people you will meet. The hundreds of students who cross your path over four years will mold you into a new person. Some will inspire you. Some will mentor you. Some will outrage you. Each will teach you a little something about the person you want to be.

Your friends, acquaintances, and classmates will become your future network for business and job opportunities. You never know if Salvador from junior-year marketing class will connect you with the hiring manager for the job you want. Or if Emily from your sorority will become a future business partner. Or if Tatiana from the intramural volleyball team will let you stay at her house for three months while you get settled in a new city.

Finally, another benefit to college is that it allows you to explore various interests through numerous clubs, activities, and groups. These offer the opportunity for a broad range of life-changing new experiences you might only have while attending college.

Keep in mind, however, that you might have access to comparable experiences outside of college. While I treasured my time at school, I found similar benefits when I traveled and worked at various seasonal locations for several years. The living situations were often a lot like dorm life, and I met great people that I'm still in touch with today. One main difference is that while I *paid* to be at college, I was *getting paid* when working full-time seasonal jobs during these adventures.

The Final Decision

If you consider and weigh the above, whatever decision you make will be the right one. As I said before, there is no wrong choice as long as you fully understand and appreciate each option's pros and cons. I suggest you use this chapter along with other resources to make the best decision for your specific situation.

If you've read this far, you are a highly motivated and focused teenager, and I have full faith in *your* ability to make the choice that will lead *you* to live your best life.

CHAPTER 27:
THE FREAKISH WAY TO DO COLLEGE

If you are heading off to college, the goal is to get you that degree and all its benefits while incurring *zero* student loan debt. To do so, you may need to make some Freakish and unpopular choices.

As a FI Freak, your college journey will look different from many of your friends' paths. You will have a job. You won't spend money on unnecessary things. Instead, you will save money and build wealth while in school. You will spend lots of time networking. And you'll do all this because it will pay huge dividends after you graduate. Making Freakish decisions while in college could get you to FI a decade earlier than if you approach those years as a "normal" college student.

If you are lucky enough to have *all* your expenses (tuition, room, board, books, fees) covered for *all* four years of school, some topics in this chapter won't apply to you. However, there are still many things in this chapter you should consider.

Most of you will not be able to pay for all your college expenses if you follow the traditional route. So let's dive in and see how a FI Freak would get through college without racking up student loan debt.

Start ASAP

Begin applying for scholarships during your junior year of high school. Set a recurring event in your phone or Google calendar to complete one scholarship application per week. Kick that up to two per week your senior year. Talk to your school counselors or postgrad office for advice, guidance, and information on local scholarships. Focus mostly on four-year scholarships.

Take classes in high school that allow you to earn college credit. AP or IB classes are great for this, and you should take advantage of them. But don't overwhelm yourself with AP or IB classes—one or two per semester during your junior and senior year is plenty.

In addition, many high schools offer various classes in which students can concurrently earn college credit. These are classes you take at your high school with other high school students. However, with these classes, you get high school credit *and* college credit at the same time—hence "concurrent" class. They differ from AP and IB options in the following ways:

- Concurrent enrollment classes lead directly to college credit.
- Concurrent enrollment classes generally do not require you to take a separate test at the end of the class to receive the college credit.
- Concurrent enrollment classes generally have no associated costs. Students simply take the college-level courses at their high school.

I have taught a concurrent enrollment marketing class to high school seniors for years. Hundreds of them have received three free college credits at a local community college while taking my class at our high school. Hardly any of my students go to the community college where they received these credits, but those credits are usually easily transferred to the college they do attend. My high school offers more than ten of these classes.

Talk to someone in your school's counseling office to see what's available. By taking advantage of both AP/IB and concurrent enrollment classes, you could start college as a second-semester freshman or even as a sophomore. I probably don't have to tell you this can save a *boatload* in college tuition costs!

Here are some other classes you should consider taking in high school for the sole purpose of preparing you for your FI journey. Check with your school counselor to see if your school offers any of the following:

- Personal finance
- Computer applications/skills
- Accounting
- Entrepreneurship
- Marketing
- Video editing (helpful with certain side hustles)

Finally, plan on going to school in-state unless you have a full-ride financial package elsewhere. Most in-state public schools have high-quality programs for a fraction of the out-of-state tuition costs at other schools. Don't waste money on an out-of-state school when it's not necessary. (We will come back to this shortly.)

Community College

Sticker prices at flagship state universities can now top $125,000 for four years of tuition, room, and board for state residents. At many selective private colleges, students who began this past fall will pay $300,000.

—RON LIEBER, *THE PRICE YOU PAY FOR COLLEGE*
@RONLIEBER

Most families never consider community colleges as an option, even though they are way less expensive than four-year schools. I know exactly why. As a teacher at a high-achieving public high school, I've seen students and parents turn their nose up at community colleges for years. They think these schools are demeaning or degrading in some way.

To this I say: *Get over yourself.*

Most community college students live at home, saving money on room and board. Plus, tuition can be about *one-third* the cost of a four-year in-state public school!

Which of these options is more important?

1. Spending four years at a well-known college?
2. Spending one or two years at a community college and then two years at an in-state public university *and* saving $40,000?

Let's give some serious thought to how much money $40,000 is.

Remember when we talked about the Big Three Expenses in Chapter Eighteen? Well, $40,000 would be more than your housing, food, and transportation expenses for two years combined. It's a *massive* chunk of change, and a FI Freak would not dismiss the opportunity to save that much.

Here are the three most likely options for college. Rather than look at them as most people do, let's look at them like a FI Freak. How do these options play into the idea of early FI for you?

1. Go to a community college (or tech school) to obtain a two-year certificate or associate degree.
2. Go to a community college for two years and then transfer to a four-year university or college.
3. Go to a four-year university or college.

Option one could be sufficient if you don't need a four-year degree to get the job you want. You might go to a technical school to become a certified plumber or electrician. Perhaps taking courses at a community college may be enough to get the certifications you need to work with computers. These are just a couple of ways you could make a substantial income only two years after high school graduation.

Option two allows you to fulfill your general education requirements in the first two years before transferring to a four-year school. This saves you two years of high tuition costs and room and board.

Option three . . . Well, let's just say be careful, especially if this option includes student loans. Remember, you're a FI Freak, and you make your choices based on your future goals and freedom, not on what everyone else does. FI Freaks make smart financial decisions now to reap decades of rewards later.

If you decide to attend a community college first, then a four-year school, here's some advice:

- Talk to an admissions counselor at the four-year school you want to transfer to and ask them what classes are best to take at a community college. Also, ask about the minimum grade point average you would need to transfer.

- Next, talk to a counselor at the community college to set up your two-year plan. While taking classes there, regularly check in with them to ensure you stay on track.
- Check out any scholarships you have received to ensure they will work with this option.

Online Degree

Another option for getting your degree is web-based education. More and more people are opting for online colleges and universities as an affordable alternative to in-person schools. You can get two- and four-year degrees, associate degrees, and certifications online. You'll still pay tuition, of course, but you won't be paying room and board and other fees associated with in-person colleges and universities.

A 2014 study by some MIT researchers and others found that online learning is just as effective as in-person learning. In addition, if you do choose to go down this road, your degree will not mention that you received it by taking online courses. Your diploma will look the same as one from an in-person school.

Classes at online schools are usually taken one at a time, and the classes can last between four and six weeks. This allows the student to focus exclusively on one course. Learning takes place in virtual classrooms in which students can use discussion boards, messaging systems, and many other resources.

Obviously, you would be missing out on some of the significant benefits of going to school in person that we went over in the last chapter. Opportunities for social interaction, clubs and activities, and networking opportunities will be much more limited. Nonetheless, online education is an option well worth considering if getting a degree is important to you.

How to Skip a Year of College

Let's suppose you've decided to attend community college first and then transfer to a four-year school. Let's also suppose you took my previous advice and earned some college credit while in high school through AP/IB classes and concurrent enrollment classes.

Here's how you can skip a year of college:

1. Take two concurrent enrollment classes while in high school. That would earn you six college credits.
2. Take two classes at the community college during the summer after your high school graduation, for six more credits. (Of course, since you're a FI Freak, you would *also* be working part-time that summer to save some money.)
3. Attend the community college during the next school year, taking a slight overload each semester. Instead of taking five classes per semester (fifteen credits), take six per semester (eighteen credits).
4. During the summer after that school year, take two more classes at the community college to earn six more credits.
5. When transferring into the four-year school, apply for them to accept two AP or IB classes you took while in high school. That's six more credits.

You now have sixty credits and are transferring in as a junior. You just skipped one year of college!

You might be thinking, "But I only saved tuition for one year of community college, which isn't a *ton* of money, because I went there for one year instead of two." And you'd be right. Still, remember the opportunity costs! You can now get your four-year degree in three years, which means you can earn full-time income during that fourth year instead of going to school full-time. Imagine the effect that will have on your net worth.

Most Expensive ≠ Best

What matters is what [you do] with your degree, not the [school] name attached to it... Strapping yourself with an extra $72,000 in debt can seriously change [your] plans for life.

—JOSHUA KENNON,
"TEACH YOUR TEEN FINANCIAL RESPONSIBILITY," THE BALANCE

Every year at my school, I see this happen to all types of students and families. They get caught up in choosing a college based on bragging rights. Some parents just can't stand the idea of telling their friends that Suzie is going to the local state university (or worse yet, community college). No, they want to be able to tell their friends Suzie is doing well at a renowned top-tier university. These parents have somehow tied their child's worth (and their own) to which college their child attends.

Please don't fall into this trap. The public universities in your state will provide you with a more-than-adequate education and experience, and they'll do it at a fraction of the cost of out-of-state or private institutions. Paying more money to go to a more expensive college does not mean you'll get a better education. What it *does* mean is that you'll graduate with more student loan debt and therefore push your FI date out years or decades. At the end of your college career, what you've learned and experienced are what that matters most.

But be warned: Private schools and expensive public schools will make it incredibly enticing to say yes to their offers. They will offer impressive amounts of scholarships, grants, and other discounts to make you *think* you are getting a great deal. However, even if an expensive school offers you 50 percent off their $50,000-per-year total expenses, the in-state public school for $20,000 with no discounts is *still the better deal*.

Bottom line: If a school is five times as expensive as your in-state public university (and fifteen times more expensive than your local community college), does that mean their education is five or fifteen times better? Of course not. It just means they've done a better job marketing their product to you and others.

Don't fall for their scheme. Remember, student loans will kill your early FI dream faster than almost any other financial decision you could make.

Pick a Promising Major

If you are heading to college, there are three important decisions you will need to make. The first is where you will go. (We hope you're considering a community college and then maybe an in-state public university.) The second is how you will pay for college. (We'll get to that shortly.) The third is what you will study.

Can we just be honest here? You've read this far because you are concerned for your financial future and probably have early FI as a personal goal. Earning a higher income will get you there faster. That's just a fact.

It's incredibly easy to find out if a future job offers high income potential or a competitive job market. Just go to the U.S. Bureau of Labor Statistics website (www.bls.gov) and search for "Occupational Outlook Handbook" and "Career Outlook." Investing twenty minutes to do this one simple thing could radically improve your FI journey.

Now, I'm not saying you should choose your college major based *solely* on the projected income or job market, but these considerations should factor into your decision. Majors like art history, music, exercise science, fashion merchandising/design, animal science, religious studies, theater, photography, multi/interdisciplinary studies, or English literature tend to have a grim outlook for earning potential and job prospects. These are the types of college majors most likely to leave you unemployed or earning less income than a job you can get straight out of high school.

I'm not telling you to stay away from those majors no matter what—if one of those pursuits will bring you happiness, then go for it. The point is to understand each option's cost and benefit and to include that information in your decision-making process. It is entirely appropriate to research your intended major, understand that it will not lead to a high-paying career, and still choose to go down that path. It's about the *knowing*. It's about looking at that information before you go down that path so you fully understand the implications of making that choice ahead of time.

If you're open to ideas, pick a major that is more likely to supply you with a high-paying job in a market with fewer applicants. Study computer science, business, nursing, engineering, finance, or software design. If those don't trip your trigger, just Google "best college majors" to find something that does.

For those of you who have no idea what you want to do but your parents demand that you go to college, I recommend having a heart-to-heart with them about where you're at with this crucial decision. Discuss the consequences we've covered and see what your parents say. Let them know you want what's best for your future, just as they do.

If after that conversation you are still heading to college without knowing what you want to pursue, I recommend majoring in business. The classes will benefit your FI journey, especially if you start investing in real estate or start your own business someday. Classes like accounting, entrepreneurship, marketing, finance, and anything having to do with real estate should help you achieve early FI.

Be a FI Freak While in School

If you go four years without generating any income, your FI journey will be significantly delayed. Finding a way to earn money and then save it (good old Mechanisms 1 and 3) while in college is the Freakish thing to do.

Perhaps you will find a part-time job off-campus or get a work-from-home gig you can do from your dorm room. It could be one of the side hustles mentioned in Chapter Sixteen that starts to earn you some extra cash. Possibly it's a full-time job you work around your community college classes. There are a lot of options, but generating some income is key.

And don't forget summer breaks. When classes end in the spring, you should have a job lined up and be ready to earn like crazy. A real FI Freak would work a forty-hour-per-week job *and* a part-time job or side hustle throughout the summer and still find ways to enjoy the time away from school. Many motivated, hardworking people have done it before you.

As long as we're talking about your Freakish approach to college, we should hit on frugality. Although we went over this at length in Chapter Seventeen, we need to quickly touch on it again. If you decide to spend thousands of dollars on formal education, you must plan on living in a way that minimizes your expenses—think frugality times ten.

The most significant savings can come from living and eating at home if you choose a school that allows you to commute. Local community colleges and public universities as well as online learning all make this possible. Some of you may want to go all in on the college experience and live in the dorms for a couple of years, and that's fine—but a FI Freak wouldn't do this unless the school was a low-priced, in-state public university.

Another way to save money is to qualify for more student aid. It never hurts to ask . . . and ask some more. Go to the financial aid office at your college (yes, in person; don't call or email) and ask how you can receive additional financial aid. I have a friend who did that one simple thing and ended up getting $2,000 in free tuition grants for the following three years. Just ask!

A final Freakish thing to do is to learn as much as you can. Take *full* advantage of the classes, experiences, internships, study-abroad programs, and other resources. If you commit years of your life to higher education, it would be wasteful to finish without having advanced your opportunities through the knowledge you've gained. Don't skip classes. Don't cheat or take shortcuts. Don't let your GPA dip below a respectable level. College is first and foremost for learning. Don't forget why you're there.

Being a FI Freak in college is not just about frugality and earning some income. It's also about continuing your journey toward early FI. The FI Freak Checklist will outline many things you should be doing during your years in college. It will guide you through self-education and tasks that will make sure you stay on track. It will even show you how to buy your first real estate property before your third year of college!

Financing

If you don't know what's going on [when considering student loans], you're about to get screwed.

—SCOTT TRENCH, *BIGGERPOCKETS MONEY PODCAST*, EPISODE 126
@SCOTT_TRENCH

Make no mistake about it—deciding whether to use student loans to pay for college is one of the most important financial decisions of your life. This is true whether you plan to achieve FI by age 25, 45, or 65. Don't screw this one up!

You need to think long and hard about the effects that student loan debt will have on you when you graduate. Hopefully you'll conclude that you must do everything in your power to avoid it. Our country is in a crisis when it comes to student loans. Hundreds of thousands of adults have student loan payments every month that severely affect their ability to live their lives and save for their future.

Many adults in their thirties or even forties are still paying off student loans. The average monthly student loan payment in the United States is just short of $400. Just take a minute and think about that. Do you want to have a $400 bill every single month for ten years after you graduate? In almost every case, it's just not worth it. Student loan payments will drastically cripple your pursuit of early FI, delaying your FI date by five to ten years!

If you *do* want to pursue that college degree, good for you—but find a way to do it *without* student loans. Goal number one should be to graduate debt-free. By using the ideas we've covered in this chapter and the resources in the appendix, you should have a great chance of achieving that goal. An even better goal would be to have some money saved up and some real assets *before* college graduation. The FI Freak Checklist will help you get there.

Hopefully, this chapter has opened your eyes to some alternative approaches to college you had not considered before. The cookie-cutter, traditional approach of one school for four years is no longer the only option, and, in many cases, it is no longer the best option either.

As you read this, you might be a couple of years from having to decide on a college education. But whether that decision is six months or six years away, take some time to look over the many resources I have put in the appendices to help you make the right choice for your future.

How you do college is a massively significant and complicated decision, yet the gravity and long-lasting impacts of this choice are often overlooked. As a FI Freak, you now know better than to gloss over this decision. Best of luck to you!

CHAPTER 28:
THE PROS AND CONS OF BEING A TEENAGER

To be yourself in a world that is constantly trying to make you something else is the greatest accomplishment.

—ATTRIBUTED TO RALPH WALDO EMERSON

Hundreds of teens make their way into my classroom every year. After getting to know thousands of them over the last two decades, I can say one thing with the utmost certainty—I respect each and every one of you.

Being a teenager in today's world is way more difficult than it was for your teachers, parents, or grandparents. The expectations are greater. There is immense pressure to earn high test scores, get into the right college, and succeed. Technology provides amazing advantages, but many disadvantages as well. Social media provides an unhealthy platform to continually compare yourself to others, many times leaving you feeling unworthy or less-than. Although the number of likes or comments generated by your most recent post is an unfair measure of value, it's hard not to care.

And all of this is in addition to the typical adolescent questions and insecurities: Who am I? What do I want to do with my life? What do I stand for? Where do I want to be in ten years? What do others think of me? Am I missing out on something? Where am I headed, and will I be okay?

I can't answer those questions for you. All I can say is you *will* get through it, and you *will* find success. I can also say with high confidence that having freedom of time earlier in life than most people will enable you to find your purpose much easier and sooner.

Your Plight as a Teenager

Here's what's gonna happen when you've decided to commit yourself to your dreams. You're gonna scare a lot of people who are comfortable around you. You're gonna scare people who don't wanna leave home. You're gonna scare people who aren't willing to take a risk. You're gonna scare people who don't believe in themselves.

—RYAN HARRIS ON THE *NGPF PODCAST*
@RYANHARRIS_68 @NEXTGENPF

As you start to envision your pathway to early FI, do yourself a huge favor: Don't believe those who tell you it can't be done or that you can't do it because you are too young. Many people have achieved FI, and the Featured Freaks throughout this book are living proof. But the typical American Dream pathway is not designed for early FI, so most people don't believe it's possible because nobody has ever told them anything different.

When faced with negative comments and efforts to discourage you on your journey, you may often feel the need to justify your intentions or even convince the cynics of their wrongness. This is *not* your burden to carry. It is not your responsibility to convince those pessimists you *do* know what you are doing even though you're young.

However, if a naysayer asks genuine questions and is truly interested in your thoughts and reasoning, give them your best answers.

You are young. Some older people will have a difficult time envisioning this type of success for you. Part of their difficulty is because of their miseducation, and part of it may be due to unconscious jealousy. Again, it's not your job to figure out why they are not enthusiastically cheering you on. Just hear their words, stand firm, and carry on.

I would tell you to *ignore* their negative sentiments, but that would be cheating you out of a valuable asset to strengthen your early FI journey: motivation. Listen to the naysayers' comments, then use them as fuel for your fire. Allow your desire to prove them wrong to push you even harder to reach your goals. Many before you have found that outside negativity can serve as the best motivator.

The Power of Starting Early

The obvious and glamorous benefit to this idea of starting sooner rather than later and harnessing the power of time in your investing is the financial success . . . But financial success is only a pawn in a much bigger, more important game of freedom of time—the ability to do what we want, with whom we want, where and when we want to.

—JERED STURM, "STARTING NOW IS GOOD, BUT STARTING YOUNG IS GREAT: HOW TIME AFFECTS INVESTING," BIGGERPOCKETS BLOG

The younger you start building your wealth, the better. When we went over compounding, it should have become astonishingly clear that saving and investing at a younger age will pay off enormously in your future. Some small sacrifices now will translate to immense wealth down the road. Dollars turn into fortunes when given enough time to grow. Implementing just a few of the strategies, concepts, and steps in this book and the FI Freak Checklist will pay massive dividends later in life. Implementing most or all the strategies will result in complete power and freedom for decades.

Always Keep a Healthy Balance

One more bit of advice: You *are* young, so don't forget to enjoy your youth. Have fun and make memories. It is outstanding that you are planning and investigating for your future, but don't lose sight of today's gifts. Don't allow yourself to get so caught up in pursuing early FI that you miss opportunities in the present.

Lunch with your friends, a weekend at the beach, a special night with your girlfriend or boyfriend, the trip of a lifetime... don't put the things you value on the back burner just to keep on a strict path to FI. That is not the point of this journey.

You will never regret spending time, and sometimes money, to make memories and enjoy experiences now, even if it pushes your FI date out a few months or years. Make sure to keep your priorities in order. Don't forget that many of those items on your happiness list from Chapter Four are things you can, and should, be doing today. Early FI, like life itself, is about the journey, not the destination. Being a FI Freak is not just about making smart *money* decisions—it's about making smart *life* decisions.

But What if It's Just Not for Me?

If you have serious doubts about whether the early FI path is for you, don't hang your head. Just being introduced to the topics covered in this book at a young age puts you *way* ahead of your peers and even most adults.

Sure, the basic personal finance concepts we've covered are essential for achieving early FI. But they are also helpful tools for *everyone's* financial future, no matter your personal goals.

Even if you decide you will not pursue early FI, this book can help you reach other financial goals in your life, such as:

- Providing for a future family
- Having the peace of mind that comes with an emergency fund
- Making intelligent decisions about college and post-secondary education
- Staying out of debt
- Using credit cards responsibly
- Building an excellent credit score
- Making smart choices with retirement investments
- And much more!

Of course, I genuinely hope you are a FI Freak who is *entirely* on board with early FI and willing to do whatever it takes to achieve it. Remember what's at stake: *decades of freedom in your future!*

What if I Start and Have a Change of Heart?

Perhaps you gave it your best shot but decided "9 to 5 until you're 65" is a better fit for you. What then? Will everything you've done and all you've learned have been a waste of time?

Absolutely not. You still will have acquired more personal finance knowledge than most people. You also will have saved some money along the way that could allow you to retire before 65 since it will have decades to grow. You will be miles ahead of anyone who chose to follow the typical American Dream path from the start. They would have chosen to spend everything they made while opting out of saving money, establishing an emergency fund, or starting to invest.

The Worst-Case Scenario

Not everyone will think the strategies and plans outlined in this book and the FI Freak Checklist are a safe and secure way to build wealth. Some skeptics may wonder:

- What if you reach FI, quit your job, and then run out of money?
- What if the stock market crashes or real estate values plunge?
- What if there's another COVID-type pandemic?

- What if things don't go the way you plan?

When someone expresses one of the concerns above, they are speaking from a place of fear. Fear is an emotion that serves a purpose—but only up to a point. Those who are too afraid to pursue early FI or warn others to steer clear are either not fully informed or can't pull the trigger themselves. (Remember the four traits of an entrepreneurial mindset from Chapter Seven?)

When people pose these fear-based questions, I usually respond, "Well, if you aren't aggressively saving money and investing it intelligently, what *are* you doing for your financial future?" I have yet to find someone who can explain a better plan to me.

Yes, things often don't go as expected in our world. This plan is designed to get you to FI at a very early age, unlocking many opportunities and options for you that others never have. Lots of research, effort, and thought have gone into this plan, and I believe it will get you to your desired goal. But no one can predict the future.

When unforeseen events (such as a recession or a pandemic) occur, *everyone's* investments take a hit. But while investing means you will be taking on the risks of a downturn, it also means you'll have a legitimate plan to grow your wealth and reach early FI. It is better to be invested for the long term and endure the occasional loss than to have nothing invested at all.

Let's imagine for a minute that your investments did lose most of their value in an economic downturn, a stock market crash, or a real estate market crash. If you were somewhere on your journey to FI at that time, it would just mean you must continue working and saving and investing for longer than you may have expected. When the economy or market eventually recovers, you will still reach early FI, just a little later than you first projected.

Let's say you had already reached FI, had quit your job, and were now living the good life. *Then* comes the downturn or crash. And it's so bad that you find your passive income and sustainable asset withdrawal are no longer covering your living expenses even after you've cut those expenses to adjust for the current situation. What then?

The answer is simple: You just do what everyone else is doing. You work. You go out and get a job to help pay your expenses until things get better. You let go of being a FI Freak (at least for a while) and just do what's normal.

In other words, *your worst-case scenario is everyone else's everyday life.*

Depending on how dire the circumstances are, you may only need to work part-time. Or maybe you can take on a lower-paying job that's more enjoyable.

In any event, don't be afraid to fail. Don't be afraid to take chances. Don't be afraid to be a FI Freak.

CHAPTER 29:
THE FI FREAK CHECKLIST

As I said way back at the start, the idea for *First to a Million* was born when one of my students asked what exactly he would need to do and when in order to achieve early financial independence.

In response, I decided to create a checklist for young people to use as they navigate the many tools and strategies of the FIRE and REI communities.

But as I started putting the checklist together, I quickly realized there were numerous basic concepts the user would need to understand first. If I didn't begin by setting a solid foundation, the checklist by itself would be useless. So the original idea expanded to include a book as well. The book is what you're reading right now. The FI Freak Checklist is in Appendix A.

Before I explain these additional resources, let's first examine some unknowns that play an essential role in their design.

Your Unknown Factors

As adults begin their FI journey, they often work backward from where they want to be to where they are now. They start designing their plan by looking at their end goal. For example, if someone who's 35 years old wants to be financially independent by age 45, they would start by recognizing they have a ten-year time frame. Then they'd plan out their journey year by year, working backward from that future point to the present. By doing this, they can map out exactly what they need to be doing each year to reach their goal.

It's not that easy for a teen. Being young, you have many major life decisions ahead that you somehow need to incorporate into your plan. You have no way of knowing if or when you'll get married or how many kids you may or may not have. You probably don't know where you'd like to settle down. You don't know what type of job you'll have or how much income that job will generate. You may not even know if you're going to attend college. Not yet having made these major decisions makes working backward a lot more complicated for you.

What if you decide to move to a different state? What if you have a child when you're 21? What if you get married much earlier or later than you expected? What if you decide you want to travel around the world for six months? What if the side hustle you start becomes incredibly successful? Your immediate future has a lot more question marks than an adult's.

That's why I created the FI Freak Checklist as a *general* guide for you. It is not a five-year plan or a ten-year plan. It's a *flexible* plan. Instead of working backward from your end goal or setting the objective of reaching FI by a certain age, use this book and the FI Freak Checklist to guide you over the next few years. If you follow the checklist precisely as I have laid it out, you will find success. But you'll probably have to adjust your plan based on the major life choices you make on your FI journey. That's okay! This checklist is designed to adapt with you as your life changes.

Your journey will have twists and turns not accounted for in the checklist. Just stay focused on the goal of achieving financial independence at a very young age and enjoying the freedom that comes with it!

The FI Freak Checklist

At its core, the FI Freak Checklist is a list of things you should do to achieve early FI. I've broken it down into four-month segments called "Freak Phases."

The FI Freak Checklist works whether you are 13, 19, or anywhere in between or beyond, and it is all you need to forge ahead on your FI journey. It will guide you with specific action items while allowing for necessary adjustments along the way. I hope it will be something you refer to regularly for the next few years.

Conclusion

At the very beginning of this book, I wrote:

Make no mistake about it: This book is not about money.

It is about freedom, choices, opportunities, and—most of all—happiness.

I hope you can now see how managing your money like a FI Freak can allow you to achieve early financial independence and live your best life.

My purpose in writing this book was to provide you with options. Until now, most young people were aware of only one option: the typical American Dream pathway of working 9 to 5 until you're 65. Now that you understand the Four Mechanisms of Early FI and the FI Equation, you have more than one option. You could follow the typical path, you could choose to aggressively and intentionally pursue early FI, or you could fall anywhere in between. You could utilize any of the numerous strategies and concepts within this book to customize your own option to fit your unique goals and aspirations.

But only *you* get to decide what is best for you and your life. Nobody else can decide that for you. Now that you are aware of the options in front of you, you get to choose what is best for you. You have complete control of how Freakish you want to get when it comes to your financial future. Financial independence awaits, so go out there and get it!

CRAIG CURELOP

⌾ @thefiguy
♪ @thefiguy

Where do you currently live?
Arvada, Colorado.

How old are you?
Twenty-seven.

How old were you when you started actively pursuing financial independence?
Twenty-three.

What was your profession/career/job when you first started pursuing FI?
I was a financial analyst in Silicon Valley making more than $100,000 per year. Sounds sexy, doesn't it? IT SUCKED! I was working eighty- to one hundred–hour weeks. My future at that company was walking forty feet down the hallway, wearing tight clothes, and pounding my chest like a wannabe Wall Street jerk.

That wasn't who I wanted to be. After some reflection, I decided that what I loved to do was travel, hang out with family and friends, and enjoy life.

My intern at the time told me about his father, who invested in a nine-unit property 25 years earlier. Today, that property is paid off and gives him $20,000 per month in passive income. That's when I first learned about financial independence.

Do you consider yourself financially independent today? How many years did it take you to get there?
I went from a net worth of negative $60,000 to financially free in just three years. Needless to say, it was a grind! I lived behind a curtain for a year (seriously). I drank very little, went out to eat very little, rode my bike to and from work…I was 100 percent dedicated to achieving financial independence as quickly as possible.

If you have reached FI, what profession/career/job do you have now, if any?
Ever since reaching FI, I have become a more active real estate agent and investor. I now lead a team

of nine agents, and we help our clients achieve financial independence through real estate investing.

Leaving my job has allowed me to take larger risks. I have increased my income ten times over, literally. Don't get me wrong. . .it's still work. But at least if I fail, I can always fall back on my investment properties.

Who or what got you started on your FI path?

My motivation to get started down the path of FI was pure hatred for my job. The idea that I needed passive income in excess of my expenses came from *The 4-Hour Workweek* by Tim Ferriss, which I still read at least once every 24 months. BiggerPockets furthered my knowledge of real estate and sent me down a rabbit hole from which I will never return.

What is your Why of FI?

My WiFi? WhyFi? First off, it's to tell dad jokes as much as possible. The more eye rolls, the better.

Second, it's to be able to live the life of my dreams and help the ones I love achieve theirs. Growing up, my parents had a massive twenty-gallon Poland Spring water jug. Every time we walked by it, we would dump our change and one-dollar bills into the jug. We called it "the Hawaii fund." Ever since I was five years old, it's been my family's dream to go to Hawaii.

As I write this, I am sitting here in Hawaii on the second of seven weeks, and my family just left after a week of their own. We created countless memories: snorkeling the reefs, climbing the tallest peak, and spending hours on the beach. Because of my financial position, I was able to pay for their entire trip. And what a small price for the time we had!

My "why" is to create more memories with my parents as they grow old (they are 60) and my future kids as they grow up. I want to have adventures with my friends. I want to grow a business that leaves a positive impact on the world. . .all of which I can do. It starts with financial independence.

What are your plans for the future?
I don't like to plan too far ahead. However, my loose plans for this year (2021) are to continue to grow the agent team and pick up a couple more rental properties. Next year, my girlfriend and I want to start our international travel. We don't know where we want to go yet, but we will go wherever our heart takes us and will do so for about a year.

What is your current savings rate?
Well over 80 percent.

If you invest in the stock market, what is your preferred type of investment or method?
Index funds.

How many real estate properties do you own? What types are they?
As of right now, I own eleven properties: one triplex, two duplexes, and seven single-family homes.

Have you ever house hacked? If so, explain. Yes! I actually wrote a book on house hacking called *The House Hacking Strategy*. I have house hacked four properties and will be looking for my fifth here in a couple of months. My first one was a duplex with one bedroom and one bathroom in each unit. I rented one and lived in the other while renting out my bedroom. Where did I live? That's where the curtain comes into play. I set up a curtain and a room divider in the living room and slept behind it for one year.

What one piece of advice would you give a teenager who wants to achieve early FI?
There is lots of advice to give. My first recommendation would be to live like a college student for as long as you can. Live with roommates. Buy a beat-up car. Make these sacrifices early on. Save that money and invest it!

You need to be consistent. You need to be disciplined. You need to be okay with being different. Keep educating yourself, reading, and listening to podcasts. Call your parents. Call your friends. Make consistent charitable contributions. Add value to the world, and the world will pay you back in multiples!

It's time to do one last check-in with social media. Record a quick ten-second video of yourself celebrating the fact that you have finished this book and are now ready to start your FI journey. Post it to all your social media accounts with the hashtags **#IMAFIFREAK** and **#TEENAGEFIFREAK**.

Don't forget to tag **@BIGGERPOCKETS** and **@SHEEKSFREAKS!**

THE FI FREAK CHECKLIST

Now that you've finished reading this book, you can use the FI Freak Checklist to guide you through the actions you should be taking over the next few years and when to take them. This checklist contains dozens of critical action steps and is all you need to move forward on your FI journey! It lays out a step-by-step plan with various tasks, like reading other books, finding a mentor, opening a brokerage account, and hitting a savings goal. The tasks are organized into 14 four-month-long Freak Phases, which together span nearly five years of your upcoming journey.

Unfortunately, no single checklist will be perfect for each and every teen. This one is meant to be a helpful guide, but it is not set in stone—you can change your course at any time and in any way, depending on your circumstances, beliefs, intentions, and ambitions. If you follow the FI Freak Checklist precisely as I have laid it out, you will find success. But most likely, you will have to adjust your path based on your personal experiences and the major life choices you make during your FI journey.

Use this checklist to guide you over the next few years, but remember that your journey will have unexpected twists and turns, and that's okay. Just stay focused on the goal of financial independence at a very young age and the freedom that comes with it.

Freak Phase 1 is meant to be completed during the summer before your junior year of high school. However, you may not be in that exact place right now. The checklist will still work for you no matter where you are in life.

Here's how to adjust the FI Freak Checklist to fit your current situation:

If you are beginning the FI Freak Checklist sometime before the summer before your junior year in high school, you can start completing some of the tasks in the first few Phases early. Then, when you reach the summer before your junior year, you can begin working on each Phase as intended.

If you are past the summer before your junior year of high school, you can play catch-up until you are on track. Try completing each Freak Phase in two months instead of four or combining two Phases into one four-month period until you are caught up. Alternatively, you could begin with Freak Phase 1 and do one phase every four months as intended, remaining a year or so behind where the checklist says you are. You will still reach FI decades before most people!

I've also created the *First to a Million Workbook*, which is available at www.biggerpockets.com/teenFI, for those who are seeking detailed, actionable guidance on their FI journey. The *First to a Million Workbook* is an interactive planner that provides step-by-step instructions and comprehensive descriptions for each of the FI Freak Checklist items.

Post–High School Plans

The most significant variable among FI Freaks is what they choose to do after high school. Some of you will decide to pursue a four-year degree. Some of you will begin working full-time as soon as you graduate. And others will choose an option somewhere in between.

There is no right or wrong choice, but what you choose will affect your ability to complete this checklist. Those who are going to school full-time will have less time to accomplish the FI Freak Checklist tasks, and that's fine—you can adjust the checklist as needed.

In opting for a four-year degree, you have already factored in the disadvantage of having less time to actively pursue early FI and decided the advantages of going to college outweigh it. Just remember that while you are in school full-time, the Phases may take longer than four months to complete.

Finally, you *cannot* sacrifice your happiness during your journey to FI. That goes against all the reasons for pursuing FI in the first place. As you advance toward your end goal of early FI, don't forget to live in the present. If you don't keep a healthy balance in your life, your motivation and ambition will fade away, leading you to abandon the journey before reaching your goal.

Now, let's get started! You got this!

Freak Phase 1

May–August

Summer before junior year of high school

- ☐ Read *First to a Million* by Dan Sheeks if you haven't already.
- ☐ Read *Personal Finance for Teens* by Carol H. Cox.
- ☐ Set three financial goals for the summer and send them to an accountability partner.
- ☐ Implement a new Freak Tweak (a creative way to be frugal).
- ☐ Sell a personal item you no longer need/want.
- ☐ Find and do a new fun, free activity.
- ☐ Go over the household bills with a parent. Set a calendar reminder to do this every month.
- ☐ Register for beneficial classes for your junior year.
- ☐ Have a parent add you as an authorized user on their credit card.
- ☐ Have a parent help you open a checking account. Download the bank's app to your phone.
- ☐ Start tracking your income and expenses using a free app.
- ☐ Get a job.
- ☐ Create goal-oriented social media accounts.
- ☐ Start a habit of listening to at least three podcast episodes every week.
- ☐ Start a habit of reading at least three blog articles every week.

Freak Phase 2

September–December

First semester of junior year of high school

- ☐ Read *Rich Dad Poor Dad* by Robert Kiyosaki.
- ☐ Have a parent help you open a savings account. Download the bank's app to your phone.
- ☐ Create an account on each of these free websites: LinkedIn, BiggerPockets, and SheeksFreaks.
- ☐ Start networking by meeting like-minded people online and at school.
- ☐ Interview someone who is where you want to be on your FI journey.
- ☐ Balance your checking and savings accounts every month. Set a calendar reminder to do this every month.
- ☐ Calculate your net worth.

- ☐ Pay yourself first at least 30 percent of your income every month. Set a calendar reminder to check this every month.
- ☐ Calculate your savings rate every month. Set a calendar reminder to do this every month.
- ☐ Evaluate who you are hanging out with (your core circle). Do they help you reach your goals?
- ☐ If you have a paycheck from a part-time job, set up direct deposit.
- ☐ Start a side hustle.
- ☐ Set three financial goals and send them to an accountability partner.
- ☐ Implement a new Freak Tweak.
- ☐ Sell a personal item you no longer need or want.
- ☐ Find and do a new fun, free activity.

Freak Phase 3

January–April

Second semester of junior year of high school

- ☐ Read *The Richest Man in Babylon* by George Clason.
- ☐ Continue networking by meeting like-minded people online and at school.
- ☐ Evaluate your income streams; add or adjust as needed.
- ☐ Evaluate your transportation costs and complete any regular vehicle maintenance as needed. Set a calendar reminder to do this every year.
- ☐ Speak to your school counselor about registering for beneficial classes for your senior year.
- ☐ Review your happiness list. Put a reminder in your calendar to do this once a year.
- ☐ Set three financial goals and send them to an accountability partner.
- ☐ Implement a new Freak Tweak.
- ☐ Sell a personal item you no longer need or want.
- ☐ Find and do a new fun, free activity.
- ☐ Interview someone who is where you want to be.
- ☐ Calculate and track your net worth.

Freak Phase 4

May–August

Summer before senior year of high school

- ☐ Read *The Millionaire Next Door* by Thomas J. Stanley and William D. Danko.
- ☐ Evaluate your income streams.
- ☐ Shadow someone for a day who does what you want to do.
- ☐ Find a mentor.
- ☐ Start a passive income stream.
- ☐ Start something that allows you to be creative while documenting your journey, like a YouTube channel or a blog.
- ☐ Review your Why of FI list.
- ☐ Set three financial goals and send them to an accountability partner.
- ☐ Implement a new Freak Tweak.
- ☐ Sell a personal item you no longer need or want.
- ☐ Find and do a new fun, free activity.
- ☐ Interview someone who is where you want to be.
- ☐ Calculate and track your net worth.
- ☐ Continue networking by meeting like-minded people.

Freak Phase 4.5

The day you turn 18 (postpone this list until your birthday)

- ☐ Get your first credit card and download its app. Set a reminder to get a second credit card when you turn 19 and a third when you are 19½.
- ☐ Open a checking account (if you don't already have one) and download the bank's app.
- ☐ Open a savings account (if you don't already have one) and download the bank's app. This will be your future investment fund.
- ☐ Start saving to reach six months' worth of expenses in your emergency fund.
- ☐ Open two more savings accounts: one for an emergency fund and one for your "fun" fund.
- ☐ Decide what percentage of your future investment fund will be for index fund investing and what percentage will be for future real estate investing. (You can change your allocations over time.)

- ☐ Open a brokerage account and start investing in a low-cost index fund.

Freak Phase 5

September–December

First semester of senior year of high school

- ☐ Read *The House Hacking Strategy* by Craig Curelop.
- ☐ Decide on your post–high school plans and whether you will be pursuing a specific career path.
- ☐ If you will pursue postsecondary education, decide what that will look like.
- ☐ If you are going to college, start applying for one scholarship per week.
- ☐ Set three financial goals and send them to an accountability partner.
- ☐ Implement a new Freak Tweak.
- ☐ Sell a personal item you no longer need or want.
- ☐ Find and do a new fun, free activity.
- ☐ Interview someone who is where you want to be.
- ☐ Evaluate your income streams.
- ☐ Calculate and track your net worth.
- ☐ Continue networking by meeting like-minded people.
- ☐ Shadow someone for a day.

Freak Phase 6

January–April

Second semester of senior year of high school

- ☐ Read *Your Money or Your Life* by Vicki Robin and Joe Dominguez.
- ☐ Help your parents with your family's annual income taxes. Set a calendar reminder to do your income taxes each February going forward.
- ☐ Finalize plans for after high school. If you're not going to college, decide what job you will pursue after graduation.
- ☐ Decide on housing for after high school.
- ☐ Make a plan/budget for income and expenses after high school.
- ☐ If you are going to college, start applying for *two* scholarships per week.

- [ ] Start building a consistent W-2 income history for future mortgage approval.
- [ ] Set three financial goals and send them to an accountability partner.
- [ ] Implement a new Freak Tweak.
- [ ] Sell a personal item you no longer need or want.
- [ ] Find and do a new fun, free activity.
- [ ] Interview someone who is where you want to be.
- [ ] Evaluate your income streams.
- [ ] Calculate and track your net worth.
- [ ] Continue networking by meeting like-minded people.
- [ ] Shadow someone for a day.

Freak Phase 7

May–August

Summer after high school graduation

- [ ] Read *The Book on Rental Property Investing* by Brandon Turner.
- [ ] Maximize your extra time this summer.
- [ ] Talk to your parents about health insurance for you after high school.
- [ ] If you are going to college, choose a major that sets you up for income and opportunities.
- [ ] Manage your expenses after high school.
- [ ] Start another passive income stream.
- [ ] Depending on your investment goals, make regular contributions to your brokerage account and invest in low-cost index funds.
- [ ] Watch the documentary *Playing with FIRE*. (www.playingwith fire.co/the-documentary)
- [ ] Set three financial goals and send them to an accountability partner.
- [ ] Implement a new Freak Tweak.
- [ ] Sell a personal item you no longer need or want.
- [ ] Find and do a new fun, free activity.
- [ ] Interview someone who is where you want to be.
- [ ] Evaluate your income streams.
- [ ] Calculate and track your net worth.
- [ ] Continue networking by meeting like-minded people.
- [ ] Shadow someone for a day.

Freak Phase 8

September–December

(If in college, first semester of freshman year)

- ☐ Read *The Simple Path to Wealth* by JL Collins.
- ☐ Find friends and social groups that share your goals.
- ☐ Reevaluate the amount you need in your emergency fund now that you have graduated from high school.
- ☐ Once your emergency fund can cover six months' worth of expenses, start contributing to your future investment fund and your "fun" fund.
- ☐ If in college, find a job.
- ☐ Start analyzing real estate investing properties. Aim to analyze five properties per week.
- ☐ Set three financial goals and send them to an accountability partner.
- ☐ Implement a new Freak Tweak.
- ☐ Sell a personal item you no longer need or want.
- ☐ Find and do a new fun, free activity.
- ☐ Interview someone who is where you want to be.
- ☐ Evaluate your income streams.
- ☐ Calculate and track your net worth.
- ☐ Continue networking by meeting like-minded people.
- ☐ Shadow someone for a day.

Freak Phase 9

January–April

(If in college, second semester of freshman year)

- ☐ Read *The Book on Managing Rental Properties* by Heather and Brandon Turner.
- ☐ Read *First-Time Home Buyer* by Scott Trench and Mindy Jensen.
- ☐ Every January, check your credit reports and credit scores. Set a calendar reminder to do this every year.
- ☐ Take your networking efforts to the next level.
- ☐ Evaluate your income streams.
- ☐ Set three financial goals and send them to an accountability partner.
- ☐ Implement a new Freak Tweak.

- [ ] Sell a personal item you no longer need or want.
- [ ] Find and do a new fun, free activity.
- [ ] Interview someone who is where you want to be.
- [ ] Calculate and track your net worth.
- [ ] Shadow someone for a day.

Freak Phase 10

May–August
(If in college, summer after freshman year)

- [ ] Read *Think and Grow Rich* by Napoleon Hill.
- [ ] Decide on the market area for your first real estate purchase.
- [ ] Determine how much money you'll need to buy your first property, and start talking to lenders.
- [ ] Reevaluate your allocations between index fund investing and real estate investing.
- [ ] Update and evaluate how well you are paying yourself first.
- [ ] Set three financial goals and send them to an accountability partner.
- [ ] Implement a new Freak Tweak.
- [ ] Sell a personal item you no longer need or want.
- [ ] Find and do a new fun, free activity.
- [ ] Interview someone who is where you want to be.
- [ ] Evaluate your income streams.
- [ ] Calculate and track your net worth.
- [ ] Continue networking by meeting like-minded people.
- [ ] Shadow someone for a day.

Freak Phase 11

September–December
(If in college, first semester sophomore year)

- [ ] Read *Retire Early with Real Estate* by Chad Carson.
- [ ] Discuss your real estate investing ideas with your mentor.
- [ ] Determine exactly what kind of property you want for your first house hack and clarify your criteria.
- [ ] Go to three open houses.
- [ ] Meet with some lenders and figure out your best financing option for your house hack purchase.

- [ ] Find the rest of your real estate team.
- [ ] Set three financial goals and send them to an accountability partner.
- [ ] Implement a new Freak Tweak.
- [ ] Sell a personal item you no longer need or want.
- [ ] Find and do a new fun, free activity.
- [ ] Interview someone who is where you want to be.
- [ ] Evaluate your income streams.
- [ ] Calculate and track your net worth.
- [ ] Continue networking by meeting like-minded people.
- [ ] Shadow someone for a day.

Freak Phase 12

January–April

(If in college, second semester sophomore year)
- [ ] Read *The 4-Hour Work Week* by Tim Ferriss.
- [ ] Choose a real estate agent for your first property purchase.
- [ ] Determine your systems for marketing your property and screening potential tenants.
- [ ] Open new bank accounts for your future property.
- [ ] Start submitting offers.
- [ ] Close on your first real estate purchase.
- [ ] Set three financial goals and send them to an accountability partner.
- [ ] Implement a new Freak Tweak.
- [ ] Sell a personal item you no longer need or want.
- [ ] Find and do a new fun, free activity.
- [ ] Interview someone who is where you want to be.
- [ ] Evaluate your income streams.
- [ ] Calculate and track your net worth.
- [ ] Continue networking by meeting like-minded people.
- [ ] Shadow someone for a day.

Freak Phase 13

May–August

(If in college, summer after sophomore year)

- ☐ Read *Set for Life* by Scott Trench.
- ☐ Find tenants and start managing your property.
- ☐ Conduct a thorough examination of your food costs.
- ☐ Update and evaluate how well you are paying yourself first. If you have steady income, set up an auto transfer to your future investment fund.
- ☐ Set some real estate investing goals.
- ☐ Set three financial goals and send them to an accountability partner.
- ☐ Implement a new Freak Tweak.
- ☐ Sell a personal item you no longer need or want.
- ☐ Find and do a new fun, free activity.
- ☐ Interview someone who is where you want to be.
- ☐ Evaluate your income streams.
- ☐ Calculate and track your net worth.
- ☐ Continue networking by meeting like-minded people.
- ☐ Shadow someone for a day.

Freak Phase 14

September–December

(If in college, first semester of junior year)

- ☐ Read *Financial Freedom* by Grant Sabatier.
- ☐ Compare rates from different car insurance companies.
- ☐ Continue to avoid lifestyle inflation.
- ☐ Get ready to buy your second property.
- ☐ Plan for the remainder of your early FI journey.
- ☐ Set three financial goals and send them to an accountability partner.
- ☐ Implement a new Freak Tweak.
- ☐ Sell a personal item you no longer need or want.
- ☐ Find and do a new fun, free activity.
- ☐ Interview someone who is where you want to be.
- ☐ Evaluate your income streams.
- ☐ Calculate and track your net worth.

☐ Continue networking by meeting like-minded people.
☐ Shadow someone for a day.

Once you complete the FI Freak Checklist, you will find yourself well on your way to early FI. There will still be more work to do, but you will have the experience, knowledge, and confidence to complete your journey. You won't be needing a checklist any longer. Best of luck to you!

APPENDIX B
ADDITIONAL RESOURCES

SheeksFreaks Community
The SheeksFreaks community is a subset of the FIRE community. The two communities are very similar, but while the FIRE community is for everyone, the SheeksFreaks community is specifically for those under 25.
www.sheeksfreaks.com
IG: @sheeksfreaks
TikTok: @sheeksfreaks
YouTube: SheeksFreaks

BiggerPockets Community
The BiggerPockets community is the largest online community for real estate investors—but it's not just for REI. There are many blog, videos, and podcasts about early FI, investing, and money management.
www.biggerpockets.com
IG: @biggerpockets
YouTube: BiggerPockets
Facebook: BiggerPockets

Other Networking Sites
- LinkedIn: www.linkedin.com
- Meetup: www.meetup.com
- National Real Estate Investors Association: https://nationalreia.org

Chapter 5: The Concept of Enough
TEDxPortland talk by Kevin Cavenaugh, "How Much Is Enough?," www.ted.com

Chapter 8: The Compounding Effect
Compound Interest Calculator, www.investor.gov

Chapter 12: Credit Cards
Best credit cards for teenagers and students:
- "Best Student Credit Cards," www.forbes.com
- "Student Credit Cards with No Credit," www.wallethub.com
- "What Are the Best Credit Cards for Teens?" www.creditkarma.com

Chapter 18: The Big Three Expenses
Resources for saving money on food:

Websites
- www.checkout51.com
- www.5dollardinners.com
- www.5dollarmealplan.com
- www.grocerybudgetmakeover.com

Articles
- "How to Slash Your Food Bill in Half," www.biggerpockets.com
- "How to Save Money on Groceries," www.ramseysolutions.com
- "15 Quirky Ways to Spend Less Money on Food," www.forbes.com
- "55 Ways to Save Money on Food," www.savethestudent.org

Chapter 20: Saving Your Money
Best bank accounts for teenagers:
- "Best Savings Accounts for Teenagers," www.bankrate.com
- "4 Best Savings Accounts for Kids," www.nerdwallet.com
- "Best Banks for Students," www.thebalance.com

Chapters 26 and 27: College
- "Graduating College on Track for Financial Independence," *BiggerPockets Money Podcast*, episode 26
- "The Ultimate College Guide: Everything You Need to Know About College in 2020," Cody Berman, www.flytofi.com
- "16 Money Skills They Didn't Teach You in High School," *Bigger-*

Pockets Money Podcast, episode 126
- "College Hacks from the ChooseFI Community," *ChooseFI* podcast, episode 230
- "How to Test Out of College While You're Still in High School," *ChooseFI* podcast, episode 238
- "The Ultimate Guide to College Hacking," www.choosefi.com
- Scholarship Mastery (four videos explaining tips and tricks many students have used to get money to help pay their college expenses), www.masteryofmoney.com

Websites
- www.sophia.org: Low-cost, self-paced courses for college credit.
- www.clep.collegeboard.org: The most widely trusted credit-by-examination program for over 50 years, accepted by 2,900 colleges and universities, and administered in more than 2,000 test centers.
- www.study.com: A flexible way to earn college credit for a fraction of the cost of traditional universities.
- www.modernstates.org: Tuition-free, high-quality courses online from top institutions for college credit.
- www.straighterline.com: Online college courses that are guaranteed to transfer to 130-plus schools.
- www.saylor.org: Free courses at Saylor Academy.
- www.accreditedschoolsonline.org: A great starting point if you are interested in getting a two-year or four-year degree online.
- www.myscholly.com: Scholly is the number one college scholarship app in the world and has helped students win more than $100 million.
- www.scholarships.com: Search more than 3.7 million college scholarships and grants.

NOTES

Introduction
The Craig Curelop quote about going against societal norms is from his BiggerPockets Blog post titled "If You're Pursuing Financial Independence, You'll Feel Different Than Everyone—and That's OK," December 18, 2018, www.biggerpockets.com.

Chapter 2: Why You Should Tell the American Dream to F Off
Results of the Gallup poll about the U.S. workweek can be found in Lydia Saad's article "The '40-Hour' Workweek Is Actually Longer—by Seven Hours," August 19, 2014, www.newsgallup.com.

Studies show that most Americans are unhappy with their current job:
- Jack Kelly, "More Than Half of U.S. Workers Are Unhappy in Their Jobs: Here's Why and What Needs to Be Done Now," October 25, 2019, www.forbes.com.
- Mark Eltringham, "Majority of American Workers Are Unhappy in Their Jobs," October 28, 2019, www.workplaceinsight.net.

Chapter 5: The Concept of Enough
Many studies indicate that once a person reaches a certain income level, their happiness doesn't necessarily increase:
- Emmie Martin, "Here's How Much Money You Need to Be Happy, According to a New Analysis by Wealth Experts," November 20, 2017, www.cnbc.com.
- Josh Hafner, "Does Money Equal Happiness? It Does, but Only Until You Earn This Much," February 26, 2018, www.usatoday.com.

- Quentin Fottrell, "Psychologists Say They've Found the Exact Amount of Money You Need to Be Happy," March 4, 2018, www.marketwatch.com.
- Dan Kopf, "How Much Money Do People Need to Be Happy?," February 24, 2018, www.qz.com.

The story of Julia Wise and Jeff Kaufman comes from Alexandra Zaslow's article "Couple Donates Half of Income Every Year to Treat World Health," October 23, 2015, www.today.com.

Chapter 6: Your Why of FI

Various studies have shown that when we serve others, we increase our own happiness:
- Elizabeth Dunn and Michael Norton, "How to Make Giving Feel Good," June 18, 2013, www.greatergood.berkeley.edu.
- Bonnie Kavoussi, "Money Can Buy Happiness if You Spend It on Others, Michael Norton Says," May 1, 2012, www.huffpost.com.

Chapter 10: Good Debt vs. Bad Debt

Statistics from Debt.org can be found in Bill Fay's eye-opening article, "Key Figures Behind America's Consumer Debt," updated January 28, 2021, www.debt.org.

Chapter 18: The Big Three Expenses

Phillip Lindsay, a Denver Broncos running back, moved back in with his parents to save money:
- Amanda Tarlton, "Top Rookie Running Back Is Living with His Parents to Save Money," November 19, 2018, www.fatherly.com.
- Nick Dimengo, "Phillip Lindsay, Broncos Stud RB, Still Lives in His Parents' Basement And Does Chores," November 7, 2018, www.brobible.com.
- Zane Matthews, "Broncos Running Back Phillip Lindsay Still Lives with His Parents," November 21, 2018, www.kool1079.com.

Chapter 20: Saving Your Money

Social media drives many to bankruptcy, depression, low self-esteem, low self-worth, and even suicide:
- Damon Beres, "10 Hidden Negative Effects of Social Media on

Your Brain," November 12, 2020, www.thehealthy.com.
- Alice G. Walton, "6 Ways Social Media Affects Our Mental Health," June 30, 2017, www.forbes.com.
- "Teens and Social Media Use: What's the Impact?," December 21, 2019, www.mayoclinic.com.

Chapter 23—Index Fund Investing and the 4 Percent Rule

More than 60 percent of Americans don't start saving for retirement until age 30 or later:
- Alicia Adamczyk, "This Is When People Start Saving for Retirement—and When They Actually Should," updated September 4, 2019, www.cnbc.com.

Brandon Turner's advice on how to deal with other people in the real estate business is from a BiggerPockets Blog post titled "5 Not-So-Great Aspects of Real Estate Investing," September 24, 2019, www.biggerpockets.com.

Chapter 26: Should You Go to College?

According to Educationdata.org, the total of all expenses for four years at an in-state public school is more than $100,000:
- "Average Cost of College & Tuition," June 7, 2019, www.educationdata.org.

The Elon Musk quote is from a *Business Insider* article by Avery Hartmans titled "Elon Musk Says College Is 'Basically for Fun' but 'Not For Learning,' and That a Degree Isn't 'Evidence of Exceptional Ability,'" March 9, 2020, www.businessinsider.com.

Some major corporations are starting to relax their requirement that new hires have a bachelor's degree:
- "15 More Companies That No Longer Require a Degree—Apply Now," January 10, 2020, www.glassdoor.com.

Chapter 27: The Freakish Way to do College

A 2014 study by some MIT researchers and others found that online learning is just as effective as in-person learning:
- https://news.mit.edu/2014/study-shows-online-courses-effective-0924.

Many adults in their thirties or even forties are still paying off student loans:
- Matthew Frankel, "Here's the Average Student Loan Payment—and How to Lower Yours," updated February 6, 2020, www.fool.com.

FIRST TO A MILLION
GLOSSARY

4 Percent Rule: The point at which you have reached financial independence—when you can withdraw 4 percent of your investments each year to pay your living expenses.

Active income: Income for which you must trade your time for money, such as with an hourly or salaried job.

Actively managed mutual fund: A mutual fund that is overseen by a fund manager who spends time picking the stocks they believe will perform the best.

Appreciation: The increase in value of an asset over time.

Asset: Something of monetary value owned by an individual. A **real asset** generates income or increases net worth. A **false asset** decreases net worth because of expenses or depreciation.

Asset withdrawal: Taking money or value out of an existing asset.

Big Three Expenses: The largest expenses in most people's lives: housing, transportation, and food.

Brokerage account: Similar to a bank account, but with a brokerage firm.

Brokerage firm: A business that acts as a middleman connecting buyers and sellers to facilitate a transaction.

Cash flow: The extra money you have left after all expenses have been taken out; usually used in reference to real estate investments.

Compound interest: Interest paid on an initial amount *plus* any previously accumulated interest.

Co-signer/Co-borrower: Someone who signs a mortgage with a real estate buyer when the buyer does not have a sufficient income history or credit score. The income history of the co-signer or co-borrower can satisfy the lender's income requirements. Co-signers don't co-own the property, while co-borrowers do.

Credit score: A numerical indicator ranging from 300 to 850 that measures your trustworthiness and likeliness to pay your bills on time. The higher the score, the better.

Day trading: The buying and selling of stocks on the same day in an effort to make fast money from short-term price fluctuations.

Debt: Money owed to a person or company, usually in the form of a loan. **Bad debt** is debt used to acquire a false asset. **Good debt** is debt used to acquire a real asset. Also known as **liability**.

Delayed gratification: The decision to resist the impulse of grabbing an immediate reward in order to obtain a more valuable reward in the future.

Depreciation: A reduction in the value of an asset over time.

Diversification: Spreading your investments over many different options to lessen the chance of significant losses—aka not putting all your eggs in one basket.

Dividends: The portion of earnings a company distributes to its shareholders.

Enough: The point at which your happiness is maximized. You have everything you need plus a little extra.

Equity: The total value you have in an investment. Equity equals the current value of an investment minus the amount you owe on that investment.

FICO score: *See Credit Score.*

FI equation: *Passive Income + Sustainable Asset Withdrawal > Living Expenses*

FI Freak: A young person obsessed with making intelligent money decisions to allow themselves to reach early financial independence and live their best life.

Financial independence, or FI: The point at which your *passive income* plus *sustainable asset withdrawal* is greater than your *living expenses* so you no longer have to work for money—also referred to as "financial freedom."

FI number: The value of stock market investments needed to satisfy the 4 Percent Rule and achieve financial independence.

FIRE: Financial Independence, Retire Early. A personal finance movement devoted to achieving financial freedom at an early age.

Forced appreciation: An increase in the value of a property due to investor actions such as improvements, upgrades, or additions.

Four Mechanisms of Early FI: Earn more, spend less, save the difference, and invest your savings wisely.

Freak: A person who has withdrawn from normal behavior and activities to pursue one interest or obsession; one who is markedly exceptional or extraordinary.

Frugality: Spending money only on things you value and not spending money on things you don't.

Gap year: A period, typically an academic year, taken by a student as a break between high school and higher education in order to explore professional and personal opportunities.

Generational wealth: Wealth that is passed down from one generation to the next.

Hedonic adaptation: The tendency to return to a baseline level of happiness despite major positive or negative events or life changes.

House hacking: A strategy where you live in one of the units or rooms of your property and rent out the rest, using your tenants' rents to pay your mortgage and expenses.

Income: How much money you bring in during a given time period. *See also* Passive income *and* Active income.

Index fund: A type of mutual fund with a large grouping of stocks that match the components of a financial market index, such as the S&P 500 Index.

Interest: The cost of borrowing money, such as the fee you pay to receive a bank loan. Conversely, interest can also be money earned, such as the set percentage a bank pays you when you put funds into a savings account.

Investing: Purchasing an asset with the expectation that the asset will provide income in the future or increase in value over time.

Leverage: The use of borrowed money to increase the potential return of an investment. The goal is to earn a return greater than the interest you paid to borrow the money.

Liability: *See* Debt.

Lifestyle inflation: The tendency to increase your spending as you make more money.

Living expenses: All the costs of day-to-day life such as housing, food, transportation, healthcare, entertainment, and insurance.

Mechanisms of early FI: See Four Mechanisms of Early FI

Mortgage: A legal agreement between a creditor and a borrower whereby the creditor loans the borrower money to purchase a property.

Mutual fund: A collection of stocks or investments grouped together so investors can easily buy shares of several companies at once.

Net worth: *See* Wealth.

Opportunity cost: The lost benefit of possible gains from other options when one option is chosen.

Passive income: Income you receive when not actively working.

Paying yourself first: Routinely and automatically putting money into savings and investments before spending on anything else.

Portfolio income: Income from investments such as stocks and bonds.

REI: Real estate investing.

Retirement account: A financial account with favorable tax treatment for holding and growing money until typical retirement age.

Return: The money made or lost from an investment over time.

Revolving debt: Debt, such as with a credit card, that the user can borrow indefinitely, provided they make minimum payments and don't exceed their limit.

Risk tolerance: Your ability to psychologically endure the potential of losing money on an investment.

Saving: Not spending all your money right away but instead putting some of it aside for later.

Savings rate: The amount of money you save divided by the amount of money you earn, expressed as a percentage.

Savings rate equation: *Money Saved ÷ Money Earned = Savings Rate*

Side hustle: A job or money-making activity you can engage in outside of being a full-time student or employee.

Stock: A slice of ownership in a company. For all intents and purposes, "stock" and "shares" are the same.

W-2 job: A job in which the hired person is considered an employee, not a contractor or self-employed. Taxes are deducted from their wages and paid to the state and federal governments on their behalf. W-2 employees receive a W-2 form at the end of the year to use in filing taxes.

Wealth: The same as **net worth**. The total of one's assets minus the total of one's debts/liabilities. Simply put, how much of your income you keep.

Why of FI: The totality of your motivations and inspirations for pursuing early financial independence.

ACKNOWLEDGEMENTS

Many people played a significant role in this book coming to fruition. First, I'd like to thank my wife and family for supporting me throughout this entire process. Next, I'd like to thank Craig Curelop and Scott Trench for their dedication to helping me spread this valuable information to young people everywhere. Thank you to my publishing team—Kaylee Walterbach, Savannah Wood, and Katie Miller—and to the rest of the BiggerPockets team. I'd also like to thank my editors, Louise Collazo and Harlee Smith, and my designer, Bambi Eitel, for their brilliant work in making this book a reality.

If you liked the book, please leave a review on **Amazon** or the **BiggerPockets Bookstore**. Your feedback means a lot to us!

A Step-By-Step Guide
To Change The Way You Look At Money Before You Turn Twenty!

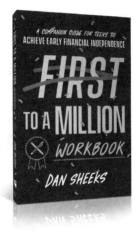

In this companion workbook to *First to a Million*, teenagers will accelerate their path to financial independence and learn even more about personal finance and investing. This interactive planner contains critical action items, tasks, and exercises—all organized into simple semester-long sections and a time-line that can be adjusted to fit your age or level of experience.

This workbook will show you how to:
- Find a mentor that can help you grow toward your goals
- Manage your expenses so you can save as much money as possible
- Get your first credit card and start building your credit score
- Build passive income streams to work toward financial freedom
- Open a brokerage account to invest in index funds
- Close on your first real estate purchase (when you're ready!)
- And much more!

It's never too early to start working toward your FI Freak goals. With time (and the compounding effect) on your side, you can win the game before it even starts!

Get the workbook at biggerpockets.com/teenFI

More from
BiggerPockets Publishing

If you enjoyed this book, we hope you'll take a moment to check out some of the other great material BiggerPockets offers. BiggerPockets is *the* real estate investing social network, marketplace, and information hub, designed to help make you a smarter real estate investor through podcasts, books, blog posts, videos, forums, and more. Sign up today—it's free! **Visit www.BiggerPockets.com.**

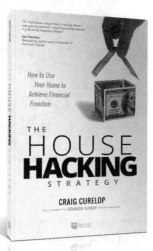

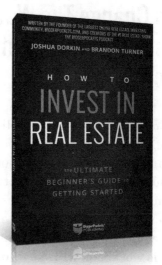

The House Hacking Strategy

Don't pay for your home. Hack it and live for free! When mastered, house hacking can save you thousands of dollars in monthly expenses, build tens of thousands of dollars in equity each year, and provide the financial means to retire early. Discover why so many successful investors support their investment careers with house hacking—and learn from a frugality expert who has "hacked" his way toward financial freedom.

How to Invest in Real Estate

Two of the biggest names in the real estate world teamed up to write the most comprehensive manual ever written on getting started in the lucrative business of real estate investing. Joshua Dorkin and Brandon Turner give you an insider's look at the many different real estate niches and strategies so that you can find which one works best for you, your resources, and your goals.

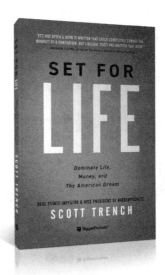

First-Time Home Buyer: The Complete Playbook to Avoiding Rookie Mistakes

Everything you need to buy your first home, from initial decisions all the way to the closing table! Scott Trench and Mindy Jensen of the *BiggerPockets Money Podcast* have been buying and selling houses for a collective thirty years. In this book, they'll give you a comprehensive overview of the home-buying process so you can consider all of your options and avoid pitfalls while jumping into the big, bad role of homeowner.

Set for Life: Dominate Life, Money, and the American Dream

Looking for a plan to achieve financial freedom in just five to ten years? *Set for Life* is a detailed fiscal plan targeted at the median-income earner starting with few or no assets. It will walk you through three stages of finance, guiding you to your first $25,000 in tangible net worth, then to your first $100,000, and then to financial freedom. *Set for Life* will teach you how to build a lifestyle, career, and investment portfolio capable of supporting financial freedom to let you live the life of your dreams.

Connect with
BiggerPockets
and Become Successful in Your Real Estate Business Today!

FACEBOOK /BiggerPockets

TWITTER @BiggerPockets

INSTAGRAM @BiggerPockets

LINKEDIN /company/BiggerPockets

 www.BiggerPockets.com

ABOUT THE
AUTHOR

DAN SHEEKS is a high school teacher, real estate investor, and personal finance advocate in Denver, Colorado. In his eighteen years as a teacher, Dan has taught various business subjects—including financial literacy, entrepreneurship, personal finance, and marketing—and worked with thousands of students. Embedded in his classes is the co-curricular DECA club, in which students travel, compete, acquire leadership skills, do community service, and have fun! His students have competed in entrepreneurship, personal finance, marketing, and hospitality services with much success at the state and national levels over the years.

In late 2019, Dan launched the SheeksFreaks community with a simple blog website and an Instagram page. The mission was simple: Provide young people with free money advice so they could live their best lives. The SheeksFreaks community is dedicated to helping young people learn money management skills to achieve early financial independence by using specific saving methods, earning extra income, and investing. The main passions motivating Dan in his endeavors are: (1) working with young people, (2) advocating for personal finance education, (3) the early financial independence movement, and (4) real estate investing.

Dan and his wife have various real estate investments, including multifamily, single-family, and Airbnb properties, as well as out-of-state BRRRRs. They currently have fifteen units in the Denver metro area, Colorado Springs, and Detroit (and they continue to grow their portfolio).

Dan volunteers in the MoneyWi$er initiative out of the Colorado Attorney General's Office with a few other hand-picked experts from around the state. The program strives to advance financial literacy in Colorado secondary education. He is also a contributing blog writer for BiggerPockets.

In his free time, Dan enjoys Colorado's many natural wonders through mountain biking, road biking, hiking, camping, and golfing. He lives just outside of Denver with his wife, Vanessa, and their son, Callum.

How to contact Dan:
LINKEDIN: Dan Sheeks
INSTAGRAM: @sheeksfreaks and @dsheeks
YOUTUBE: sheeksfreaks
EMAIL: dan@sheeksfreaks.com
WEBSITE: www.sheeksfreaks.com